Solid Rock - *by Mike Capron*

Real Cowboys
Grand Canyon to Mexico

Ed Ashurst

Ed Ashurst Publishing Company
Douglas, Arizona

ളൂᘓ
Dedication
ളൂᘓ

This book is dedicated to Leann, Emilee, Miles, Cristee, Allison, and Grant. Maybe someday they will read it, and then they will understand their granddad better.

Table of Contents

Real Cowboys
Grand Canyon to Mexico

Introduction

ഇറ

*The worst part of holding the memories is not the pain.
It's the loneliness of it, memories need to be shared*
Lois Lowry

The cowboy has been, for the most part, misrepresented by writers who don't know their subject and actors who are poorly directed. There are a few good volumes out there: *Trails Plowed Under*, *The Log of a Cowboy*, *They Pointed Them North*, and others. My personal favorite writer is J. F. Dobie, and his book *Cow People* is a masterpiece. My friend Mike McFarland wrote a good book, and I mention him in this book. Joe Brown has done a good job of describing cowboys of the twentieth century, as did Stella Hughes in her book *Hashknife Cowboy*. But authentic books about real cowboys are rare.

These stories are true and written about people I know, many of whom I worked with. I was present when most of the things I describe took place. I may be criticized by some for mentioning a thing or two that would be better left unsaid. My purpose isn't to make anyone look bad, but to give a realistic picture of life on a cow outfit.

I have tried to describe people more than events. A colorful sunset, a good looking horse, a beautiful girl are a wonderful sight, but an interesting personality is a treasure in itself.

I hope I can take you there, and make you see the people, and get a glimpse of the richness of their character. This book is about them, not me. I was just lucky enough to be there watching and listening while living below the poverty line on cowboy wages. I've paid my dues, and I feel like I have the right to tell the story.

Ed Ashurst
August 3, 2013

I've been tamped full of BS about cowboys,
Known as a wild nomadic band.
Bold knights of the saddle,
They round up wild cattle,
And roll cigarettes with one hand.

Opening stanza of "The Cowboy's Ledger"
Written by Uncle Ben

෨ඏ
Foreword by Fred Fellows
෨ඏ

I was having that last cup of coffee in the morning before going to feed the horses and roping steers. The telephone rang and it was Ed Ashurst. We got the customary "Have you had any rain?" out of the way when he asked me to write a foreword to this book. To me it was like Billy Graham asking the choir boy to write next Sunday's sermon. Something I've never done and I was not sure I was qualified to do it. I read Ed's book *Miracle or Coincidence* and I found out that Ed is as articulate and talented a writer as he is a top cowboy and rancher. Having read the manuscript to *Real Cowboys*, I feel really honored to write this foreword.

Two of my favorite books are *We Pointed Them North* by Teddy Blue Abbott and *Log of a Cowboy* by Andy Adams. Abbott's and Adams' books are about trail drives in the 1870s from Texas north. Ed's book is about cowboys and ranch people during modern times. Like Teddy Blue and Andy Adams, Ed's stories are true and written by a man who's been there. They are a modern day history about cowboys and ranch people that Ed has worked with; people that will be preserved in this book forever.

In my 45 plus years on the art road in the west, I've been lucky to have gone out, slept in a teepee, worked cows and stayed with the wagon; the Padlock, O6, and the Haythorne to name a few.

I started out working for Butler Saddlery in Paramount, California. While working at the saddle shop one day a man came in and offered me a job punching cows on the Jameson Ranch at Tehachapi, California. It was a working cow ranch owned by the Monolith Portland Cement Company. It was a great experience and I was in heaven. One day my step father called and asked

me if I wanted to go to work for Northrop Aircraft in Hawthorne, California, as an artist. I told Smokie Bethal, the cow boss, about the offer and he said, "If it was me, I would do it." I got my pay and rolled my bed and headed for Los Angeles. I worked at Northrop as an artist for seven years before going out on my own to paint full time. It changed my life forever, but my heart is and always will be with cow people. Joe Beeler said one time that every artist wants to be a cowboy and every cowboy wants to be an artist. That was sure true for me and still is.

That's why this book appeals to me so much. It is about a life I missed out on while pursuing a 50 year career in art. Even though painting and sculpting has been my main endeavor I thank GOD for team roping on weekends and spare moments so I can stay horseback and keep my hand in.

Onetime, while on the wagon at the Sarpy Creek Division of the Padlock in Montana, Royce Hanson, the wagon boss, said if you get down to Arizona look up Ed Ashurst. I didn't know Ed when we moved from Bigfork, Montana, to Sonoita, Arizona. Then one fateful day, Deborah and I decided to go down to the Sonoita Fairgrounds to watch the Ranch Rodeo Competition. I took my camera and looked forward to a pleasant day. As the ranch teams gathered for instructions, one cowgirl who rode for her ranch in New Mexico called out, "HELP! Our ranch cowboy's truck broke down in Lordsburg and what are we going to do?"

My wife Deborah (bless her) said, "Fred will fill in for him."

I said, "Hey, I don't have a horse here."

From the back of the bunch of cowboys and horses came a voice, "You can use my horse."

I said, "I don't even have my rope."

"You can use my rope," came from the same cowboy. You guessed it, it was Ed Ashurst!

To make a long story short, I borrowed his horse and rope. On our first steer, I roped him and got him and our horses in the trailer in the middle of the arena. We were leading it. I've always heard that a man is known for the kind of horses he rides. Four of the best horses I've ever roped on were Jack Roddy's Soapy and my three head horses, Brownie, Blue and Trim, the horse that Trevor Brazile rode when he set a world Team Roping record at the NFR in Las Vegas. I think Ed's horse was as good if not better than any of 'em. That tells me that Ed knows what he's doing in every department. Ed's too humble to agree but I've heard from cowboys north and south that he's one of the best ropers, wild cow catchers and wagon bosses in the country. I was going say that his reputation comes by easy, but that would be wrong. The reputation as a top cowboy does not come by easy. Ed has cowboyed for 50 years on the Babbitt, Yolo, Muleshoe, 7-UP, O RO and was wagon boss on the Diamond A, arguably Arizona's biggest ranch. What Ed says about cowboys and ranch life, you can take to the bank.

Contrary to what some people think, the cowboy is not dead. You can't see cattle gathered and worked in rough country from the freeway or out of a United Airlines' window. There are men and women working cattle in the vast reaches of the West almost always out of reach of cell phones. This book *Real Cowboys* is about those men and women, some passed on and some still living.

Their stories will live on in this book forever.

In addition to ranching Ed has been President of the Arizona Cowpunchers Reunion Association four times and served on the board seven times. Today, he's managing the Ten X Cattle Company, a working cow ranch on the border east of Douglas, Arizona... that could be a whole story in itself!

I can't wait for Ed's next book, and I'll wager after you read this book *Real Cowboys* you will be waiting for Ed's next book also.

Fred Fellows CA
Member of the Cowboy Artist's of America 45 years
Three Times President CAA

Frank at CO Bar Ranch, circa 1960. Photo courtesy Ed Banks.

Frank Banks

Many who are self-taught far excel the doctors, masters, and
bachelors of the most renowned universities.
Ludwig Von Mises

T he modern world, in which we now live, has become ho-
mogenized. Because of television and the endless reach
of the internet, we have become one people, a worldwide
puree of faceless humanity that is devoid of any singular character or local flavor. The kids in Brooklyn dress and act just like
the kids in El Paso. Blue jeans that are seven sizes too big and
worn low enough to expose the crack that people used to hide
have infiltrated into the farthest outposts of the frontier. Indi-
viduality has died and mediocrity prevails. Not so in the good
ole days.

Frank Banks was a cowboy of note whose career of fifty-
odd years ended when he retired as Babbitts' ranch manager in
1969. Frank owned a hard-earned reputation of being a very
competent ranch manager and cowman that was built upon the
fact that he was first a good cowboy. He was well liked by his
contemporaries and had the reputation of being fun loving as
long as it didn't interfere with serious business. He was un-
questionably honest and loyal to both employer and friend. But
like so many of his generation, he was eccentric, especially in
comparison to mainstream civilized man. Honed by years of en-

during the hardships of cowboy life amidst prolonged drought, severe blizzards, too much work, and too little pay, he acquired a delicious peculiarity that suited him fine. Unlike most specimens of twenty-first century manhood, Frank didn't care what others thought of him; he had a life, a job to do, and a direction that he was headed.

Frank was born in Oregon in 1910, where his father and uncles were in the logging business. His father was a skilled teamster who owned a large remuda of work horses that he worked in the logging trade. When Frank was around seven years old his father and uncles pulled up stakes and moved to the Los Angles area in Southern California, but the elder Banks was not happy there, and he soon moved to the desert of southwest Arizona near Salome.

Several years later when Frank was nine years old, they packed up and moved again, this time to the Hart Prairie area near Flagstaff. During this move of several hundred miles, Frank was heavily involved in moving his father's large herd of horses, which included mares and studs and broke draft animals. At times Frank was left alone to move the horses as well as tend himself, in spite of his young age.

When he was 15, Frank went to work for Babbitts on what was then known as the Pitchfork Ranch south and east of Flagstaff; Kilo Pruitt was the wagon boss. After several years he went to work for Charlie Young on Babbitts' CO Bar Ranch north of Flagstaff.

Around 1933 Frank and the CO Bar crew were camped at Kendrick Park at 8000 feet elevation on the northwest corner of the San Francisco Peaks. There had been a severe drought throughout Arizona for some time, and Babbitts had moved 500 cows from their W Triangle Ranch north of Ashfork to the CO Bar because of the lack of feed and water on the W Triangle. The W Triangle cows were mixed with the CO Bar cows on the west end of the CO Bar in what was, and still is, known as the Double Knobs pasture. One afternoon Charlie Young told Frank to take an extra horse and leave Kendrick Park and go north to Cedar Ranch, a cow camp 12 miles distance. The Double Knobs country was drying up and the CO Bar cows knew by instinct to go east and find water, but the W Triangle cows wanted to go west where they had come from, and they were walking the fence and drying out.

Frank saddled a horse, and also caught a horse called Granite that he knew was tough, and leading Granite headed toward Cedar Ranch, arriving there after sundown. After feeding his two horses he lay down in the log bunkhouse and went to sleep. Around 1:00 a.m. Frank awoke and made himself some coffee,

Frank Banks - *by Mike Capron*

and after a cup or two he saddled Granite and started loping west to a dirt tank called Little Wild Bill fifteen miles away, which is in the southwest corner of the Double Knobs Pasture. He started his drive traveling north on the West Knobs fence gathering W Triangle cows as he went. It is 10 miles north of Little Wild Bill to the northwest corner of the Double Knobs Pasture, and by the time Frank got that far he had most of the 500 W Triangle cows gathered up and moving in front of him. From the northwest corner of the Knobs, you go east-northeast 11 miles to a big dirt tank called Lockwood, which was one of the few waterholes that still had water. Frank had a fence on his left side to keep the cows throwed up against that was undoubtedly a big help, and single-handedly he trailed the 500 dried-out cows to Lockwood and a much-needed drink. From Lockwood it is 14 miles back south to Cedar Ranch. Frank and Granite had left Cedar Ranch at 3:00 a.m. and they got back at 2:00 a.m., 23 hours later. He never stopped on that trip except to dismount and relieve himself. After an hour's sleep, he saddled up, and leading Granite, made it back to the wagon at Kendrick Park in time to catch a fresh horse and help the crew gather some more cattle.

Frank was a tall lanky man who never packed much excess weight, and in his prime was as hard and tough as the root of a mesquite stump. He had a voice that belied his rugged appearance, being high and shrill when he spoke, which only added to his singleness of character.

Frank was a storyteller and appreciated a captive audience. He had a unique way of keeping them captivated. After a long discourse he would stop, unexpectedly, and stare at the person listening, asking, "Do you believe that?"

Without fail the person would reply, "Yes, Frank! Sure I believe that!"

Then he would really test you. "What do you believe?" he would ask? Frank expected you to pay attention when he was talking!

In the summer of 1974, a bunch of us Babbitt cowboys rounded up and branded some colts that Frank was pasturing near Redlands on the W Triangle Ranch. We worked hard all morning, and by noon we were finished and retired to the Redland's bunkhouse for some lunch and refreshments. Frank had already consumed a quantity of Seagram's VO in celebration of his good colt crop. He was wanting to tell stories.

In a pasture called Little Redlands, which goes west from the camp, there was a large bunch of geldings that were turned out for the summer. In this bunch was an old mouse-colored horse that was obviously very old. His face had become quite roan with the white hairs of old age. The horse's name was Claudia, and no one could remember how old he was. Frank and I were visiting and I asked him, "How old is ole Claudia, Frank?"

He replied, "Well, I tell you what, Ed, I was right there at Cedar Ranch in 1937 when ole Tom Connell started Claudia, and he was a three-year-old. I was right there and saw the whole thing in 1937."

"Wow!" I replied. "That would make him forty years old, wouldn't it?"

He looked at me as if dumbfounded, "Well, just figure it out for yourself, Ed. Just figure it out for yourself!"

Frank with a stud called Naco purchased from the O RO. Photo courtesy Ed Banks.

During the same conversation Frank told me a story about working on Babbitts' Pitchfork outfit when he was about 18 years old. He and the rest of Kilo Pruitt's crew were chasing some wild steers on Anderson Mesa about a mile east of Ashurst Lake. Frank rode up on a grave that had been molested by some treasure hunters looking for buried gold. My grandparents, William and Sarah Ashurst, owned that country before Babbitts, and established the ranch in the 1870s. Their ranch house was about one-quarter mile away near a spring called Ashurst Run. Their fourth child, Margaret, who would be my great aunt, died of diphtheria in March of 1879 when she was several months old. William and Sarah buried her, and put up a large engraved headstone, and a nice fence around the grave. William was rumored to be wealthy, and distrustful of banks, and was said to have buried gold at various spots near the Ashurst cabin and surrounding area. Many articles have been written in treasure magazines about the Ashurst gold buried on Anderson Mesa. Somebody, only several days before Frank discovered the molested grave, had dug it up; no doubt, looking for the famous treasure that probably doesn't exist. The fence around the grave had been knocked down and the headstone turned over. "It was the most pitiful thing I ever saw, Ed!" Frank said, repeating the statement several times in his high-pitched voice. In 1997 I was cowboying in that country, and I found the grave complete with the beautiful headstone that had been set upright, but the fence was gone.

Like all good cowboys, Frank loved horses but might have had a different interpretation of what one was. For many years the Babbitt Ranch, under Frank's management, supplied the bucking stock for the famous All Indian Pow Wow and Rodeo held on the Fourth of July. For the most part these broncs were part of the ranch's brood mare band. One story goes that a well-known Indian bronc rider stepped onto the back of the bucking chute to strap his riggin' on the bronc he drew and looked down and saw the W Triangle brand on the mare's shoulder. He lifted his bareback rigging off the mare and retreated to parts unknown muttering something to himself about not getting on one of those *+#*^* W Triangle horses.

Frank Banks (left) and Slim Kite (right) with a friend during the 1930s. Photo courtesy Ed Banks.

Ben Fancher ran onto Frank in Flagstaff one time and the two had time to visit for awhile. Ben had worked for Frank and the two knew each other well. "How's the horses doing out there, Frank?" Ben asked.

"Good, Ben, good!" Frank replied. "We killed three Indians at the Pow Wow this year!" Winning the NCHA Cutting Futurity wouldn't have been any sweeter.

Frank took over as manager of the W Triangle Ranch in 1937, and then Babbitts made him manager of the CO Bar Ranch as well. Unlike many modern day managers, who manage from an office and computer, Frank continued to run the cowboy crew and cow work; as well as make management decisions. He considered the two tasks inseparable, an opinion that every good ranch manager I've known has agreed on.

The Coconino Plateau, where the lion's share of the two outfits is located, is great cow country, but historically has always been short of water. When Frank took over running the outfit, livestock water was acquired chiefly from a few earthen dams, or what Arizona cowboys refer to as dirt tanks. Even these were small compared to the dirt tanks that are scattered over the range today, due to the fact that ranches today have access to quality heavy earth-moving equipment. When Frank was a young man most of the dams were built with teams of mules pulling fresnos, hardly an equal to a modern D8N Caterpiller or 966 loader. What few wells existed were shallow and subject to go dry during the frequent drought situations. Under Frank's management somewhere between 75 and 100 miles of stock water pipelines were laid carrying water to hundreds of sections of pastureland. Several million gallons of water storages were erected and dozens of good water troughs. Frank seemed to have a knack for finding a site for drilling a good water well, and wells that were drilled under his management are still used today. Several good cow camps, complete with a decent home for a married cowboy, were built at strategic yet remote areas of the ranch.

Frank took the Babbitt cattle operation from the primitive pioneer days well into the 20th century, and he kept it cowboy, continuing to work cattle from the back of a good horse. He never acted or played the part of a big shot but continued to live with, and interact with, the men who worked for him. His sense of humor remained intact, especially his ability to act it out physically as well as mentally.

Bill Howell went to work for Frank in October of 1963. Bill told me that a month or so after going to work for Frank the Babbitt crew threw a big roundup together near Buck Tank on the W Triangle Ranch. They had four or five hundred cows in the herd and they had a considerable amount of cutting to do. Bill ended up between the roundup and the cut and was staying busy turning back as Frank cut cattle by him. On the back side of the herd was a well-known cowboy named Frank Cain, and he was mounted on a three-year-old bronc named Uvalde. Uvalde would still buck people off 11 years later when I went to work for the outfit. Frank Cain was a tad bit scared of Uvalde and wasn't real keen on riding him.

After Frank Banks had cut cattle out of the herd for a half hour or so, a big fat dry cow weighing about 1300 pounds broke out of the herd and tried to run off. Frank Cain took after her and tried unsuccessfully several times to turn her back into the herd. The cow wouldn't cooperate so he roped her with a tied rope. The cow outweighed him and Uvalde by a couple hundred pounds. Bill watched from the opposite side of the herd as the cow jerked and drug Frank Cain and the bronc all over the place. Bill said he thought about going out and heeling the cow for Frank Cain, but he would have had to ride around several men to do it, and beings he was new to the outfit, he wasn't sure if that would go against protocol. The rest of the crew acted like they didn't know what was going on, even though the battle that was taking place was impossible to ignore. Frank Cain was too scared of the bronc to deliberately hit the end of the rope hard enough to knock the cow down. Bill was sure Frank Banks could see what was taking place but acted like he hadn't noticed.

Finally, after another forty minutes had passed, Frank Banks finished sorting and rode out of the herd toward Bill. When he got within talking distance he snapped his head around in mock surprise and looked at Frank Cain and Uvalde, who were still engulfed in a cloud of dust. "Well, looky there, Bill!" acting as if he had just noticed. "There's ole Frank Cain out there and he's got a big ole cow roped on that poor little colt. Well, that's the most pitiful thing I ever saw. Bill, that's the most pitiful thing I ever saw!" Frank went on, speaking in his high-pitched voice, "How 'bout going out there, Bill, and help poor ole Frank get loose from that cow."

Cain and Uvalde - *by Mike Capron*

Frank might have met his match when he met his wife Helen. When they were living at Anita on the W Triangle, some friends had come over to visit and they were all sitting down and eating together. Helen told Frank that she had baked his favorite pie, and when it came time to serve it, she sat the pie pan down on the table in front of Frank. She had a second pie pan turned upside down on top of the one that supposedly held his favorite dessert. Helen told Frank the lid over the pie was to keep it warm. Frank lifted the pie pan up to his nose in anticipation. He lifted the lid, which was now only inches from his nose, and saw a small dead prairie rattler that Helen had neatly coiled where a pie would have been. Frank destroyed the table as he tried to escape his favorite dessert and wasn't seen for quite a spell. Helen didn't care because it took her an equal amount of time to get over her convulsions of laughter.

Jack George gettin' his skillet tamed - *by Mike Capron*

Jack George

O! Let me not be mad, sweet heaven;
Keep me in temper; I would not be mad!
William Shakespeare

Jack George came from central New Mexico and was born in the 1890s. I have worked with a number of old-timers who knew Jack when he was a young man in the vicinity of Hot Springs, presently known as Truth or Consequences. Among them were Buck Smith and Raymond Scott; Leland Larson and Johnny Mullins were also in that area when they were young as well as Burley and Elmer McDonald. In those days, according to Buck Smith, whom I worked with and for, and for whom I had immense respect, Jack had the reputation of being a good hand and was well liked; although a bit cantankerous at a young age.

Sometime in the 1930s Jack migrated to Northern Arizona and stayed there the rest of his life. He remained a bachelor and always worked on ranches. He was by reputation a good cowboy, but the older he got the more he found work as a cook. Also, the older he got, the more cantankerous he became, and seemingly followed mood swings like bends in a river, leaving any companion he might have wondering what would come around the next bend.

One winter Jack and several other men, including Carl Welsh who told me the story, were holed up at Black Tanks on the 3Vs. Jack was cooking and the other men were supposed to be gathering remnant cattle that had been missed during the fall roundup. There came a big snow and then another, and the crew became snowed in with nothing to do but wait out several weeks of bad weather. Several weeks turned into a month or more and Black Tanks was, and still is, an isolated place. I know because I've stayed there myself. After a few days, Jack started getting quiet and bowed up. While the other men sat around and did nothing but play cards and drink coffee, Jack continued to cook, and everyone got a full dose of cabin fever. Finally, Jack quit speaking completely and existed in a cloud of vitriol that would kill a boy, or an old man that was sick.

One morning he was frying steak in a big cast iron skillet on top of a very hot wood stove, and as he attempted to move the frying pan with a bare hand, he grabbed the utensil, burnt himself, and dropped it on the wood plank floor while cursing profusely. A quick thinking cowboy immediately jumped up and grabbed a six-shooter that was hidden in his bedroll, and emptied all six rounds into the cast iron skillet, and screamed an oath exclaiming that no *#/*^#!# frying pan was going to hurt a friend of his and get away with it. The frying pan was ruined, but within minutes Jack was smiling and talking as if he had never been happier in his life.

One time Jack was working at the O RO and was cowboying instead of cooking. The crew was camped at Mohon gathering cattle in the late fall. They were making a drive into Palominos Tank, and Whistle had dropped Jack off in the middle of Palominos Canyon. Someone had made Jack mad and he had been bowed up for several days. Whistle Mills, the wagon boss, and several other men had made it into the holdup right at Palominos Tank and had a small herd of cattle held up there waiting for the rest of the crew to come in. Whistle looked up the canyon and saw Jack coming down the draw following several head of cattle that seemed to be gentle. When Jack got about a hundred yards from the tank, he took his rope and went to whipping the cattle he had been following and managed to get them running, and when he reached the holdup he had them stirred up enough they blew right out the other side with Jack in hot pursuit screaming like a banshee. He managed to run everything off despite the efforts of the other men trying to get them stopped and under control. Evidently, Jack wanted everyone to know he was out of sorts.

According to legend, Jack worked for Frank Banks on the Babbitt Ranch a total of eighteen times. Frank thought the world of Jack, as did most of the other old-timers I knew that were acquainted with him. The men his age seemed to overlook his voracious appetite for hateful deeds. I knew a good many younger men who didn't approve of his crazy mood swings.

Jack George scattering the hold up - *by Mike Capron*

One spring Jack had been cooking for the Babbitt branding wagon, and as far as anyone could tell, things had been going fine. They were camped at the Tubs when they finished the roundup about the last day of June. Frank always had a company draft book and paid all the extra help off and sent the steady employees back to wherever they were going to camp for the summer. There was talk among the men about getting together in Flagstaff to celebrate the Fourth of July. Jack told Frank that he was going to stick around camp for several hours so he could clean the place up and put the stuff away, and the two men, who were friends, agreed to see each other soon. As soon as Frank's pickup was out of sight, Jack put a large sauce pan on the stove and filled it with shortening and bacon grease, and when it got hot enough to be liquid, he poured it down the sink. He then took what was left of the wagon's supply of eggs, which was several dozen, and cracked them all over the kitchen floor. On his way to his pickup he took the time to take an axe and chop the propane line in two. He then got in his vehicle and drove into Flagstaff, which was 40 miles away. He was ornery!

Several years after that episode, Jack was cooking for the Babbitt roundup crew again. Bill Howell was living at the Redlands Camp and running the cow work for Frank while they were working cattle on the W Triangle Ranch. Jack had developed a particular dislike for Bill, possibly because he was at that time a newcomer to Arizona: the fact that Bill was younger and a better cowboy than Jack didn't help. Their relationship got so bad that Jack refused to speak to Bill, or even acknowledge he existed. The cow work required that the cook needed to bring them a lunch in a pickup almost every day. Sometimes the spot where the lunch was to be delivered would be 10 to 15 miles away, and could be different than the day before. Because of Jack's refusal to communicate, Bill devised a plan: he would make a comment in the morning to one of the men in the crew that would go something like this, "I think we will eat lunch today at Red Dyke about eleven o' clock." At eleven o'clock the cook and lunch would show up, but Jack refused to admit he had taken orders from that damn Bill Howell; who, Jack would tell people, had enough meat on his head to stew a sack of onions!

I met Jack in the spring of 1971. I landed in Prescott looking for a job, and while hanging around his feed store, Art Savoini told me that Marion Perkins had just been in looking for a cowboy and had told Art that he would return in an hour or two. Directly, Marion showed back up with Mike McFarland, who was his foreman, and a fellow from Broken Bow, Nebraska, named Gar Holbrook, whom they had just hired down at the employment agency called the Palace Bar.

Marion hired me and I followed Mike and Gar out north of town, and when we got to Chino Valley, we turned east on Perkinsville Road. We crossed the Verde River at Perkinsville and traveled on north to a cow camp on Marion's Bar Cross Ranch that was called Sand Flat. Sand Flat was pure Arizona with an old wooden barn that had seen better days, and to one side were a horse corral made out of cedar pickets and a round corral made out of cedar. The house was an old clapboard two-room shack with a corrugated tin roof. The room to the south was a small kitchen, and through the antique wooden door you entered a room with two iron bedsteads and a little extra floor space, in case the population swelled past two individuals.

Jack George was in the kitchen, and Gar and I were introduced to him while he was informed that he had two extra mouths to feed. On the kitchen floor, and everywhere else, was a busy little Chihuahua-cross dog that I soon learned was Jack's favorite possession, and he answered to the name of "Tyke."

It was late in the day when we got to Sand Flat, so after doing a few chores that were minimal, we ate supper and soon after that we turned in for the night. Jack occupied the bedstead nearest the kitchen door, and Mike had his bed rolled out on top of the other that was across the room. There was a nice open corner, which held a considerable amount of unneeded space, and Gar was told he could roll his bed out there. Nothing was said to me, but, through a simple process of elimination, I deduced that my bed would have to be in what was left of the middle of the room directly in front of the door leading outside. I thought about rolling it outside, but I didn't want to be unsocial so I chose to make the best of the situation and try to "fit in" if that was possible. I was definitely the "kid" of the outfit, or to be more exact, I was the resident gunsel, tinhorn, or greenhorn, and odd man out, all rolled into one. I was painfully aware of my lack of expertise and experience as a real bonafide cowhand, but I needed a job, and I was going to try to tough it out and be somebody.

The room was dark except for the view one could get of the stars when you laid in bed and gazed through the numerous cracks in the walls of the house. I lay on my bedroll staring through the cracks, and before long I was visited by Tyke, Jack's Chihuahua dog, who pretty much had his way around the house. The dog wanted to be my friend, and repeatedly licked my face and lay on my pillow; and just about the time I thought he would be still long enough for me to go to sleep, he would jump up and scamper off in chase of a mouse or an imaginary intruder. This process was repeated several times, and then one of my roommates got up and stumbled over the top of me to get to the door and step outside to relieve himself. And then the cowboy would stumble over me a second time, grunting with displeasure at the nuisance of having someone sleeping in front of the door. About then Tyke returned to finish cleaning my face and, subsequently, another man with a full bladder made his way over me and to the door. I suppose it was one thirty in the morning when I went to sleep.

About 4:00 a.m. I was awakened by the sound of Jack banging around in the kitchen cooking breakfast. I was laying on my right side and could catch a glimmer of Coleman lantern light coming through the crack under the door between the bedroom and kitchen. Tyke was sound asleep laying an inch or two in front of my lips, and I lay still for a spell listening to the hiss of the lantern as it made its light. I wondered if a man was allowed to rise early and join the cook for a cup of coffee, but I could tell that Mike and Gar were sound asleep so I thought I had better be quiet. I was stiff and I thought if I rolled over perhaps I could go back to sleep for a few minutes. Trying to be quiet I rolled over, and when my head came to rest on the end of the pillow that I had not been using, my cheek landed on something cold, wet, and slimy. That dog had taken a big crap on my pillow! The realization of it hit me like a hammer, and I turned, and knowing exactly where the no good little turd hound lay, I reared back with my right hand and swatted him as hard as I could, launching him through space, and splattering his worthless little body into the kitchen door.

"Bow wow, wow, wow!" Little Tyke howled as loud as a forty-pound lion dog and cried puppy tears as he did it. There was a thunderous movement of molten magma in the kitchen, and then Jack kicked the door almost completely off its hinges and appeared in the doorway holding the lantern high with his right hand and in his left was the freshly sharpened blade of a 14-inch butcher knife.

"What the hell is going on here?" The question was not screamed, but merely spoken, and was like the red-hot breath of Moses as he questioned the multitude about the golden calf. Mike and Gar were sitting up in bed, so startled after being wakened by the visage of certain eternal judgment about to be delivered in the form of a shiny blade, they were rendered speechless.

Jack was now staring at me with gritted teeth, but I was bold and was not going to be forced to provide a lavatory for the cook's dog. "Your dog crapped on my pillow!" I replied loudly and with as much indignation as I could muster. Jack took three or four steps forward and held his lantern to shed light on the crime scene. All three men shifted their focus to the locality of my offense, and then I, too, looked down and saw, not a dog turd, but the remnants of a steak bone that little Tyke had drug up there in the night.

"Huh!" Jack grunted, and then he turned and went back into the kitchen. Evidently there was no honor in cutting the throat of a gunsel so dumb that he didn't know the difference between a dog turd and a bone.

Ed Ashurst on three-year-old colt. Oaks and Willows February 1972

ℰⱭ ℭℛ

The O RO Ranch

ℰⱭ ℭℛ

Ah but a man's reach should exceed his grasp,
or what's a heaven for?
Robert Browning

On the first Monday in September of 1971, which was Labor Day, I drove up Walnut Creek, crossing the old iron girder bridge close to the K4 headquarters, and turned up the creek toward the "Grant." I was hoping to get a job with the O RO wagon that I knew would begin their fall roundup soon, if they hadn't started already. After passing through the aluminum gate at the boundary of the Grant, in those days it was unlocked, I drove on toward the Oaks and Willows, which the O RO headquarters was called. A mile or two past the aluminum gate, the road passes by a dirt tank called Seep Dam, and about there my 1963 Ford pickup gave up the ghost.

I was on my hands and knees on the top of the pickup's radiator staring at the carburetor when a Jeep Wagoneer with four elderly people drove up and stopped. A handsome old gentleman with wavy gray hair and a kind-looking smile approached me and my sick vehicle and inquired if I needed some assistance. I think he knew by intuition that my mechanical ability was nonexistent. I told him I had hoped to find the ranch headquarters and ask about a job, and he introduced himself as Charlie Greene and explained to me that he owned the outfit. I introduced myself as Ed Ashurst and we shook hands. He smiled and asked me if I was any relation to Henry Ashurst, the senator, to which I explained that the senator was my great uncle. He seemed to be pleased and told me that Henry Ashurst had done his family a great service many years earlier. The Mexican government, during one of their many political upheavals, had stolen vast land holdings and assets belonging to the Greene Cattle Company in Sonora, Mexico. My great uncle Henry had, at their request, used his political connections to negotiate with the Mexican government, and as a result they retrieved a part of the fortune the Mexicans had stolen.

Charlie offered to give me a ride to the Oaks and Willows several miles away, so I got in the Jeep Wagoneer with Mrs. Greene and a couple whose names I don't remember, and we left my crippled pickup behind. Upon arrival at the Oaks and Willows we found Whistle Mills, who was the wagon boss, along with Buck Smith, Ed Evans and Jack Jones all inside the barn sorting horseshoes. The atmosphere was quite casual, and everyone seemed at ease around Charlie Greene who introduced me to Whistle, informing him I was looking for a job. Whistle asked if I had a bed and saddle, which I did. Then he asked me if I would be willing to ride young green horses and seemed pleased when I said yes. With no other questions, he hired me.

Charlie Greene's father started ranching in Cochise County around Tombstone in the late 1800s, but became famous for developing large copper mines in Sonora, Mexico. His influence and renown traversed both sides of the United States border with Mexico, as well as the financial district of Wall Street. Colonel Greene, as he was known, at home with Mexican miners, Arizona cowboys, and Yankee financiers; in his spare time put together one of the largest cattle ranches in the world. The O RO Ranch in Sonora stretched from Agua Prieta to Cananea and took in hundreds of square miles and employed hundreds of people.

The Colonel's children, of which Charlie was the youngest, came north to Yavapai County in the 1930s and bought the Baca Float No. 5, widely known as the Grant. The Grant is a 144 square mile piece of ranchland northwest of Prescott. A year or two later, the Greenes acquired an additional six townships of deeded and state lease land laying west of the Grant.

The Baca Float No. 5 is one of the five parcels of land that were originally claimed by a family called Baca, who were an old Spanish family from New Mexico. They had a deed for a Spanish Land Grant given to them that totaled 20 townships in size. The United States government didn't want to honor that claim of ownership, especially for a piece of land that large, so the Baca family hired attorneys to represent them, and an agreement was finally made. The government agreed to give the Baca family five parcels of land, each being 12 miles square, with some freedom as to where they would pick and choose those sites. Those five parcels, two of which are in Arizona, were called Floats. The Grant, or east side of the O RO Ranch northwest of Prescott, was known as Float No. 5. For obvious reasons, a transaction of this magnitude required numerous attorneys, real estate experts, and surveyors, which turned out to be very unfortunate for the Bacas.

Charlie Greene told me a story one time about the fate of the Baca family. Charlie's wife was known as Sandy to people close to her, but her given name was Margarethe. Her maiden name was Tittman and her father, whose name was Edward, was a well-respected attorney in New Mexico. They lived in Hillsboro, and when Mrs. Greene was a young girl she had a friend whose name was Baca, and she was one of the only descendants in the family who had laid claim to the Baca Land Grant. The Baca girl told the Tittmans that dishonest lawyers and real estate speculators stole all of the Baca land holdings, leaving the Baca family broke. Charlie Greene told me this story claiming that it was true and I believed him.

Within two days of my arrival at the ranch, everyone who was going to be working with the wagon assembled at the Oaks and Willows with the exception of the Bear Creek and Francis Creek men who would join the crew in a day or two. Whistle Mills, the wagon boss, was 75 years old. He was a small man, weighing maybe 145 pounds, and had snow white hair. He wasn't a man who was loud or quick to anger; actually, in the year and a half or so I worked at the O RO, I never saw him raise his voice toward man or beast. He would keep a clean pair of Levis and a shirt rolled up in his bedroll, folded in a certain way, which enabled him to put them on with the look of being freshly pressed and starched. He was always clean shaven.

Ralph Chapman, the cook, and Whistle had been friends for 50 years, and for a short time in the 1930s, had been partners on a ranch at Bear Flat 20 miles north of the town of Bagdad. I asked Ralph why he and Whistle dissolved their ranching business, to which he replied, "We drank up the profit." Ralph was originally from Chicago, and when he joined the Army as a young man, he had been sent to the trenches on the Western Front where he had received more than his share of German mustard gas. The army patched him up good enough to send him back to Chicago where a doctor informed him he wouldn't live over several months because of the severe damage his lungs had received from mustard gas. The doctor also told him in an off-handed way that the dry climate in Arizona could raise his life expectancy another six months. Ralph moved to Prescott and lived another 53 years. He was a little guy with a chest that looked like it had caved in. He smoked roll-your-own cigarettes made with Velvet tobacco and brown cigarette paper. Ralph was a reader and owned a small library, and also had a library card from the public library in Prescott. He would get cranky and sulled up on occasion, but was never loud, although he could make precision cuts with his tongue when he chose to. For the most part he was good natured and delighted in testing someone's intellectual perception by listening to their responses to his subtle and witty remarks. The only person he ever treated with open animosity was his friend Whistle, and on occasion they would fight like old married people. Ralph was clean and, for a man, was as good a wagon cook as any I've known, only being equaled by Raymond Holt and perhaps Buck Moorehead.

The best ranch cooks I've known have all been women. I've eaten after several really bad ones of both sexes, but the worst by far was a specimen known as "Goat Blair" who cooked for Mike Landis at the Double O wagon south of Seligman. Charlie Gould and I loaded Goat in a pickup and dumped him out on the sidewalk near the Black Cat Saloon in Seligman, threatening mutiny if Goat remained on the payroll. We stayed and Goat didn't.

The O RO had the most pleasant bunkhouse at the Oaks and Willows of any ranch I ever worked on. There was a big kitchen and dining room with several adjoining bedrooms in the main structure, and off of that, on the east side, was an addition with a large bathroom and then four small bedrooms, all of which were entered off of a long screened in porch. There was a small fenced-in yard with grass and trees, and while I worked for Charlie Greene this was all kept in good repair. It wasn't new or fancy, but it was very clean and comfortable.

Ralph and Whistle both had their own rooms, these being two of the four that emptied out onto the nice porch. Each of the rooms had a small wood stove, and if occupied by one man, there was room for a piece or two of furniture. Every night Ralph Chapman would lay on top of his bed, would hold a book up in the air over his head, and would read while lying flat on his back. There was a chair very close to the bed with its back next to the wall. Whistle would enter Ralph's room, sit in the chair, and smoke Camel cigarettes while Ralph would read his books. Many times I passed by the room with the door open and observed these two friends of fifty years, one lying flat and the other one sitting, and usually they were both silent. A lone light bulb hung from the ceiling illuminating the cigarette smoke that hung thickly in the air as the two coexisted for a few minutes, or perhaps an hour, needing each other without knowing it.

The O RO remuda consisted of about 80 geldings, all of which were bays, browns, sorrels or chestnuts. There were no palominos, grays, roans or pintos. (The first winter I was there I broke several black colts, but that would come later after my first roundup working there.) The O RO at that time acquired a reputation of being an old man's outfit because most of the steady hands were, in fact, in their 60s or 70s. Younger cowboys seemed to avoid permanent employment there, and because of this they were having trouble getting their young horses broke, and they had plenty of them. I was greener than fresh spring grass, but I was strong and too dumb to be scared; and I wanted to be a cowboy, which to me meant you could break a horse to ride and rope a wild cow. Because of these attributes, if they could be called that, I soon had 14 horses in my string and all but two of them were 4 years old or younger. Everyone else in the crew had seven or eight horses. Actually, I had too many because I wasn't getting them rode enough to do much good. But they kept asking me if I would like to try this one or that one, and they would rope and drag another one out to me, and I would get on them and ride off. For the most part, the colts were gentle and had good minds on them. Because of the dearth of steady hands who would ride young horses the O RO had for several years sent their young horses off the ranch to be started by a trainer named Rick Currens, who would start them at his training stable in town. I rode lots of these colts that Rick had started. Many years later someone asked me if Rick had done a good job breaking the O RO horses, to which I had replied, yes, he had. After thinking about my answer for a minute or two, I told the person who asked the question that I needed to rephrase my answer and say that the colts he started all knew a lot more than I did, and I wasn't sure how good a job he had done.

The O RO was about 350 sections, or square miles, in size, and when I worked there they told me there was between three thousand and thirty-five hundred cows on the ranch. The crew consisted of 10 cowboys, a horse wrangler, and Ralph, the cook. We started the fall roundup in 1971 at Francis Creek and finished off at the Grant the day before Thanksgiving. We did not take a day off from start to finish.

Whistle had been running the wagon for about seven years when I went there. He had spent his entire cowboy career within a hundred miles of the outfit and had at one time or another worked on most of the outfits in the vicinity. He had spent a lot of his time on the Yolo Ranch, the Triangle HC and the 7 Up and was a legend among those who told stories of gathering wild cattle.

We worked with what is called a holdup, which means in essence that you have someone waiting in place at the spot you want to gather your cattle into, perhaps a water hole or corral,

O RO Crew left to right: Ed Ashurst, Jerry, Ed Evans, Buck Smith, Roy Olson, Ringo McCoy and Coley Lyons at Pine Springs, Fall of 1971. Photo courtesy of Roy Olson.

or maybe just an open spot in the middle of a thicket. Whistle would scatter his crew out, and everyone would try and steer the cattle they gathered toward the holdup spot where, hopefully, the cattle would be stopped. The drives would be small and many times you would only gather a half dozen head of cattle, but when things were going right, that first bunch could be used as a nucleus that you could build upon. After the first drive or circle, the holdup might be moved to another spot, probably not too far away, and several men would be left with the small herd or "holdup" while the rest of the crew scattered out and gathered a new piece of country, driving the cattle into this holdup. Usually there was very little fence to control the cattle, and because of this, you had to learn to be ahead of a cow and control her. It wasn't as simple as getting behind and following fast cattle, and many times there would be more men in front than behind a bunch of cows. The cattle that were being held by the holdup men were padding for the new ones to be run into: so if the cattle wanted to be wild or run off, they could be stopped more easily when they were chased into a bunch that had already settled down. This process of making small drives into a holdup might be repeated four or five times in a morning, making the herd grow bigger with each drive.

After gathering as much country as the wagon boss wanted to, we would be ready for the noon change. The horse wrangler would bring a change of horses, one for each man, and we would hold them up in a makeshift rope corral made up of three or four men holding their ropes in between each other, and the fresh horses would be roped by Whistle, and everyone would eat a quick lunch that Ralph would bring from the wagon in an old Willys Jeep. The wagon and camp would usually be several miles away. You would change horses and eat three or four men at a time while some of the crew stayed with the herd of cattle we had spent all morning gathering. You would get a new horse and eat quickly and then get back to the herd to trade with someone who had been holding herd.

After "nooning-out" we would "work the herd." Whistle would position one man away from the herd, while everyone else held the cattle in place, while he or someone of his choosing would ride in the herd and cut out whatever cattle needed separated. When a critter was cut out, the man who was stationed off by himself would stop them and hold them separately from the main bunch. This was called holding the "cut" and was generally thought of as a lowly job intended for the less capable cowboys. Actually, it was quite important and like everything else there is a right way and wrong way to do it. When the herd work would first get started in the afternoon, and there were only one or two critters to hold, it could take more cowboy ability to do so than anything else that happened in a day. If someone failed to hold the cut and let them run off, the entire crew would be angry because the entire day's work would be lost.

Big calves that were going to be shipped would be cut out, as well as yearlings, or old cows and bulls. After everything had been cut out of the main herd, any unbranded calves that had been gathered would be branded. Usually there would be a corral of some kind to assist in all this work, but occasionally it would all be done outside. The herd would always be worked out in the open. When all of this had been accomplished the cut would be trailed to a holding trap somewhere. Most of the time the wagon and camp would be set up somewhere near this holding trap.

This process, of gathering a piece of country, sorting the cows, and trailing the cut to a holding pasture would be repeated day after day. The first day of the roundup we would start in one corner of the ranch, and the next day we would work the country that lay adjacent to the country we had worked the first day, until eventually the entire ranch had been gathered one small piece at a time. A big herd or roundup put together in a morning's work at the O RO would be 100 or maybe 150 mature cows plus calves, yearlings, etc. Some days you might only gather 25 or 30. The country was rough mountainous country, and in places thick with pine, juniper, cliff rose, mahogany, algerita, and other types of brush. There was lots of water, and lots of places for a cow to hide or try to escape from a crew of cowboys. There were plenty of opportunities to rope a critter that was trying to escape and remain in the wild.

The man who was second in command on the outfit was Buck Smith. Buck had originated on a ranch near Engle, New Mexico, east of present day Truth or Consequences 20 or 30 miles. He was 65 or 66 years old in 1971 and was still a strong active man. He had worked for the Greenes in the mid '30s when they first bought the ranch, and then after a brief hiatus finding employment somewhere else, they hired him to manage their ranch at Naco in Cochise County. When the Greenes sold the Naco Ranch, he moved up to the ranch north of Prescott. Buck had the demeanor of a true servant and was available to help anyone or everyone on the crew with whatever need they might have. He would help you shoe a colt, set up your teepee, or chop wood for the cook. He cut the hair of many a cowboy who had been a long time away from a town and a barbershop. He was Whistle's jigger boss, and although Whistle had few equals when it came to handling cattle in rough country, Buck was a better cowman. Buck never questioned Whistle's authority and the two men respected each other's opinion. Buck was the man who seemed to take the most interest in the O RO horse program and was the one who promoted me into position of head colt rider for the outfit. There was a lot of things I didn't know about riding green horses, but beings I was all he had to work with, he kept putting me on them and turning me loose. He was very good to me. Buck's real name was Emory and Whistle's name was Elton, and occasionally they called each other by their given names, but to everyone else they were Buck and Whistle.

Another old-timer on the O RO was Coley Lyons, who stayed at the Triangle N Camp at the foot of Mohon Mountain on the east side. Coley was also in his mid 60s and had worked for the Greenes for nobody knew how long, probably 35 years or so. He was a nephew of Oscar Coleman, who had managed the outfit 30 years earlier. Coley, like Whistle and Ralph Chapman, was a lifelong bachelor. He was probably the best camp man I ever saw anywhere I worked, before or since. He not only took care of the Triangle N country, but also the country on the west side of Mohan Mountain, as well as a pasture called West Split. He packed lots of salt and had a better handle on what was going on around a huge portion of the ranch than anybody. He liked and took care of his horses, but would wear out a lot of horseshoes, and his horses all had lots of saddle marks on their backs because he used them hard.

One time in December they sent me and another fellow with a pickup load of salt to Mohon Camp, which is west of the Mohon Mountains. We left the Oaks and Willows very early, figuring we would catch Coley in camp and give him his mail before we went on around the mountain with our load of salt. It was a bitter cold day with a strong wind, and we got to Triangle N way before it was getting light, probably around 5:00 a.m. Coley was gone, but there was still a fire in the wood cook stove and evidence that he had been gone only a short while. We left his mail on the kitchen table and went on toward Mohon Camp, which was probably 15 or 16 miles by the road that goes around the mountain on the north side. We stacked the ton of salt blocks in a small shed at Mohon, which would enable Coley to pack out of there, depositing salt at various salt grounds on the west side of the mountain. About noon we ran onto Coley along the road several miles north of Mohon Camp. It was still cold, probably about 35 degrees, with a 30 mile an hour wind. Coley had been in the saddle since way before daylight and was headed the

Coley Lyons in the door of the saddle house at the Oaks and Willows. Photo taken by Ray Swanson

opposite direction of camp toward some unknown destination to check on something that he thought needed checking on. We visited for a minute or two and then he went on, obviously too busy to visit with a couple of buttons who had nothing better to do than deliver salt while riding in the warm cab of a Dodge truck. At the age of 65 he was still motivated: perhaps growing up during the Depression had left him with a fear of starving to death, but whatever the reason was, the man was motivated.

Coley was probably 5 feet 9 or 10 inches, but like Whistle and Ralph, he wasn't packing any fat. He was actually a frail looking man, but he was proof that looks can be deceiving. He worked with the wagon, but the rest of the time, which was 6 or 7 months out of 12, he worked by himself. There was no telephone or two-way radio, and weeks would go by with no one checking on him. He had been living that way for years and it suited him fine. When roundup started Coley was talkative and friendly, but by the end of the roundup he was quiet and obviously ready to go back to camp. He had a custom built pair of spurs made by Ed Blanchard with Chihuahua shanks. He had made the rowels himself out of brass, cutting each spoke with a hacksaw into the shape of a snowflake. The rowels were probably two and a half inches in diameter and rang so loudly you could hear him coming a long way off.

In mid December after the wagon had pulled in, six of us gathered a pasture called Cow Creek, which was located on the northwest corner of the Grant. There were three or four hundred yearling replacement heifers running in there, and they had been there since spring. The crew consisted of Whistle, Buck, Ed Evans, Jack Jones, Joe Smith who was Buck's son, and me. When Whistle and Buck counted the heifers out the gate, we were about 80 head short, and though we looked for them, we never found hide nor hair of them. Although I didn't learn about it until several years later, there were several steers missing from a neighboring outfit at the same time. Like the O RO heifers, the steers were never found.

There were, at the time, a couple of rough customers living in the country, and most everyone was afraid of them whether they would admit it or not. The cattle inspector was a cocky little Banty rooster who liked to strut around on shipping day, and give orders to the cowboys he had no authority over, and generally act important. Had either one of those hombres looked cross-eyed at the inspector, he would have wet his pants and made himself invisible real pronto. Thirty years after the disappearance of these cattle one of the men, who is a friend of mine, admitted to me that he was involved in the theft; he even described in some detail how it was done, and how they slipped the cattle out of the country.

After the O RO crew, including me, got the heifers gathered out of the Cow Creek pasture, we started them toward the Francis Creek Camp, which is on the southwestern corner of the ranch, and over 28 miles of rough trail to reach. We stayed the first night at the Triangle N Camp with Coley Lyons, and Whistle cooked as good a pan of biscuits as I ever tasted. The second night we stayed at Bear Creek Camp, and reached Francis Creek the third night. Along with the replacement heifers, we also trailed all of the extra horses that weren't going to be used during the winter and turned them loose near Francis Creek. Everyone except me rode some of these extra turn-out horses, but I had two that I needed to ride back to the Oaks and Willows. The night we arrived at Francis Creek, there came a big snow accumulating six or eight inches at Francis Creek, which was the lowest elevation on the ranch. The snow was as deep as 18 inches on other parts on the Grant. The fourth morning of our journey we loaded our beds and camp outfit on a Dodge Power Wagon and everyone, with the exception of me and Ed Evans, got in the truck and headed toward the Oaks and Willows, 32 miles away. Ed and I saddled the two colts that I was going to ride all winter and headed north following the Dodge truck. It was a cold overcast day, and I remember the sun being filtered through the clouds made the landscape look a crystal blue color. Ed and I trotted into the Oaks and Willows about sundown.

The first of January, we gathered eleven colts for me to start, 10 three-year-olds, and 1 four-year-old; I started 4 in January, 4 in February, and 3 in March. I rode them all in a hackamore, and would ride them three or four rides in the round corral, and then go outside. All 11 of them had been ridden at least 25 times by the end of the winter, and some of them a lot more than that. I worked my tail off riding colts and put lots of miles on them, but probably didn't teach them much, except how to deal with a lot of sweat under a saddle blanket.

The first of April the outfit hired two new cowboys; their names were Twister Heller and Bob Scott. Twister and Bob were three years older than me, but a full millennium ahead of me in experience, and I soon realized I had a great deal to learn about riding young horses. Within a few days of their arrival, Bob and I were riding a couple of the colts that I had just started. We were out a ways from camp riding through some cows when Bob said, "Let's rope a cow." Without waiting for me to reply, he built to a two-year-old heifer and stuck it on her. Wow! I thought to myself. I didn't know you could actually rope on a horse this green. Before too long, I found out Bob could do lots of stuff that I couldn't do.

Buck asked me to turn in seven of the eleven colts I had started through the winter and keep whichever four I wanted. They gave Bob four of them, and Twister three, and I kept the four of my choosing. They sent Bob and me to stay with Bill Walker at Francis Creek so we could help gather and scatter bulls and gather the remuda that had been turned out there all winter. It was the first week of April, and we were going to stay there helping Bill until the wagon and roundup crew joined us around the first of May. The spring roundup would start at Francis Creek, the same place as it had the fall before.

One of the colts I had started that winter was a little mouse-colored horse called Toddy. I kept Toddy in my string when I was asked to turn seven in to mount Bob and Twister. Toddy had bucked hard several times but hadn't bucked me off. Several days after Bob and I got moved to Francis Creek, I stepped on Toddy, and he threw me off within a jump or two. We were in a big wire lot that lay between the house and the creek bottom. I lay on the ground and watched the colt buck down the fence toward a corner with a double H brace made out of big cedar posts, with the top wire about 50 inches off the ground. "He's going to kill himself!" I thought as I lay there watching, but instead, when he reached the corner with its stoutly made H

Toddy jumping the fence corner - *by Mike Capron*

braces, he jumped over the fence touching nothing as he did so. The jump that cleared the fence was no different than the one before or the one after. "I better get a handle on this situation," I was thinking to myself.

Francis Creek Camp sat at the bottom of a canyon right at the spot where the canyon narrows and gets deeper. Above the camp the canyon widened out and you could travel horseback any direction you wanted. To the northeast you could see the southern edge of the Mohon mountain range several miles away. Down the creek the canyon walls immediately rose sharply with the black malpai rimrocks at the top of the canyon walls, making it impossible to climb out of the canyon except where a few tributaries flowed into it. Coming down from a mesa west of the camp, there was a steep road that came to a gate near the creek bottom on the south side of camp. One morning I led Toddy through this gate. My plan was to mount the colt amidst the large boulders in the creek bottom because I had heard lots of old-timers say a bronc won't buck hard if you get him in a big rock pile. Bob Scott was already mounted and watching from where the road hit the canyon bottom. Just like the old-timers said, I took my bronc to the middle of the biggest boulder pile I could find, and my choices were endless. Some of the rocks were as big as small cars or pieces of machinery. As the old cowboy saying goes, "I had him in my pile." I stepped on and realized some of the information old-timers give you isn't based on good intelligence. Toddy bucked out of the rock pile heading for the bottom of the steep road, as Bob rode ahead ready to catch him if he became "loose," or what some people call "riderless." We were traveling up the steep road faster than I had planned, and about half way up I realized both of my feet were in the vicinity of my left stirrup, and my head was near my right stirrup, and my belly in my saddle. My bridle reins were dragging the ground but, by golly, I was still on my horse. Somehow, I managed to set myself straight in the saddle and gather up my dragging reins. When it was over Bob and I had to stop so he could get down on the ground and rest. He was tired from laughing so much. I stayed mounted.

Whistle, Buck, and all the rest of the wagon crew showed up at Francis Creek a day or two before the first of May. We spent a day or two shoeing the remuda and then went to work. In those days the O RO did not wean any calves in the fall with the exception of 30 or 40 percent of the steer calves, which they would sell in the fall. The rest of the calves stayed on their mammas until spring, and the cows did most of the weaning the natural way. In the spring each day, when we were through gathering in the morning, we would throw our roundup together and cut out the yearlings. Many of these were still attached to their mothers, even though for the most part they were weaned. Most of the cows would have new babies on which to direct their attention. But the yearlings, nonetheless, would not appreciate being separated from their mothers or familiar surroundings. All of this made for a lot of expert cowboying, for to handle a bunch of yearlings in rough brushy country, when the yearlings aren't happy with the program, can make life interesting. After getting the yearlings separated from the herd, we would brand the new calves or anything else that was unbranded. Finally, after getting the branding done, we would trail the yearlings to camp and put them in a holding pasture. Everyone had to be on their toes, and be ready to plug a hole, and be in the right place to keep the yearlings under control. Getting the opportunity to rope a runaway yearling was commonplace. We repeated this scenario day after day, and there was plenty of excitement if you were someone who enjoyed that type of work.

Around the first of June, we were camped at Cottonwood at the foot of Mount Hope on the west side. We made a big drive starting at Buck 'em Off Flat and going into Oak Dam where there was a good big waterlot and a smaller corral to brand in. This drive was one of the bigger drives of the entire roundup, and we gathered a big bunch of cows, probably around 200. Before branding we cut out a 130-something yearlings and penned them in the big waterlot that surrounded the dam and water hole. We penned the cows and babies in the smaller corral.

After getting the calves branded we left them and their mothers penned so we could have all the crew available to get started trailing the yearlings to a holding pasture that was four or five miles away. After getting the herd started, someone could slip back and let the cow and calves out of the branding pen. Whistle took Bob Scott and me out of the gate ahead of the cattle and told Bob to take the left point and me to take the right. He would stay in the lead. We were expecting the cattle to come out fast and be a bit skittish, but were not expecting what happened next. The waterlot and dam sat in somewhat of a hole, and there was a small hill just outside the gate that blocked our view from what was going on, beings we went out a short distance past the hill in order to give the cattle some room to see and take the gate. Suddenly, the yearlings came over the top of the hill running full blast and you could tell by the look in their eyes they weren't going to slow down anytime soon. There was a certain character in the crew who had a peculiar way of riding. He would put his right hand on the top of the saddle horn, and while sticking his right elbow out, he would roll both of his shoulders back and forth in a swinging motion as his horse would trot. He was noted for being slow when he should be moving fast. When the yearlings came boiling over the hill in a dead run, Whistle, Bob and I went with them, staying in front, trying real hard to keep them collected and somewhat under control. When the first 30 or 40 topped the hill running full speed ahead, we looked back and saw this cowboy trotting along in the middle of the herd with yearlings running wildly on all sides of him. He was swinging his shoulders and had a big smile on his face with a roll-your-own cigarette coming out of one corner of his mouth. It almost seemed as if he was thinking to himself, "Wee, Wee, Wee! Look at them go! Look at them go!" I have no idea how the man got in the middle of the herd, which is sacrilege, or why. I suppose he didn't know either. But being there made the cattle run faster, and run they did.

The herd of yearlings ran, and ran, and then ran some more, and all we could do was try and keep them together, and going, somewhat, in the right direction. Finally, after a mile and a half or so, we got most of them stopped. A couple had to be roped, and a couple, no doubt, got away, but we managed to keep most of them captured. Roping in a situation like that is usually counter productive. A cowboy might get three or four tied down, but when a hundred and thirty are getting away, it's better to sacrifice the few to save the many. The cowboy with the rolling shoulders never knew anything out of the ordinary had taken place.

There was a small piece of country on the Grant that had not been gathered for seven or eight years. Whistle's story was that he had not felt like he had the right kind of crew to gather it, and so for a long time they just glanced off the edges, so to speak, but never really got into the heart of the area. This piece of country was southeast of the Oaks and Willows four or five miles, and lay against the eastern boundary of the Grant, and took in the Dairy and Bear Mountains. Whistle and Buck knew there were some wild cattle in the area, just because it had been neglected for so long, but no one knew for sure what was in there.

We had started roundup a week or two earlier than usual, and because of that, we finished at the end of the third week of June. Whistle and Buck decided to take a small crew up onto Dairy and Bear Mountains and try to gather as many cattle as they could. The plan was to work in the area for five or six days. Whistle took Bob Scott, Ed Evans, Buck Smith and his son Joe, and me with the idea we would drive what we could off the mountain and catch and tie up critters that didn't want to cooperate.

The first morning we worked up there, we got up to Dairy Spring, which lay in the bottom of a saddle between Dairy and Bear Mountains at about 6500 feet in elevation. There were lots of big yellow pines and juniper and oak trees, as well as varieties of chaparral such as cliff rose and manzanita. There were not many flat spots or clearings bigger than a small house. We snuck up close to the spring and split up with plans of surrounding it, if possible. No one was talking and we moved quietly as possible. I was fairly close to Whistle, and just as the sun started showing on the mountain tops, he stopped and pointed toward the spring fed water trough, and peering through the trees, I could see four head of cattle drinking; it looked like two mature cows and a couple of bull yearlings. We stopped momentarily and then someone's horse stepped on a branch, and the faint noise caused the cattle to jerk their heads up and turn towards us, perhaps they could smell us, and like four head of deer they were off to the races.

The cattle scattered four ways at first, and then in the rush of the excitement, I lost track of what was happening except the whereabouts of the bull nearest me. One of the bulls headed straight south on an old trail, and I could see Whistle in hot pursuit riding his horse, ole Turdhead, who was a big bay with no white anywhere on his body. Turdhead's registered name was Nada Nada, which is Spanish for nothing, because of his lack of white hair. In mixed company, Whistle, who was always a gentleman, didn't want anyone saying Turdhead, and the horse would instantly become Nada Nada. The bull I was after crashed through the brush going west, and I managed to turn him south on the same trail Whistle was on in pursuit of the other yearling. I had to plow my way through some thick vegetation to keep up, but I found the trail and my bull was a couple hundred feet ahead of me. Whistle was directly ahead of my bull by another hundred yards, and he was swinging his rope about to catch his bull when he went out of sight over a little rise in the trail. The bull I was chasing, as well as me and my horse, were in Whistle's tracks going as fast as horses and bulls run. When I topped the little rise that had momentarily hidden Whistle from my view, I looked forward perhaps a hundred feet and saw Whistle wrapping his pigging string around his bull's hind legs. I raced past him and roped the other bull about 50 yards down the trail. This whole process had taken about a minute to unfold. Whistle had, at the ripe young age of 76, caught the first critter of the day. Buck Smith had roped one of the cows and Bob Scott the other. They were unbranded three-year-old cows and the two bulls were yearlings weighing about 650 pounds.

We tied the cattle to trees with Whistle giving instructions how to do it, having first tipped their horns with a saw. He later gave instructions on how to lead one, teaching mostly by example as he insisted on leading as many as possible, which was quite a few because we were having some success at catching them. Whistle was in his element during this week of wild cow catching and, except for his looks, seemed to be 40 years old instead of 76.

On one of the days we were on this wild cow chase we ended up on top of Bear Mountain, which was thick with trees and brush. We traveled from the east end to the west and didn't jump anything until we were near the west end where the country starts to descend at a steep angle. There were 8 or 10 head of cattle in a bunch and they took a run off the side of the mountain. About three-fourths of the way down to the saddle in between Dairy and Bear Mountains, we got the cattle held up. The oak brush was thick enough to conceal a great deal of what was hidden in the shadows of the vegetation. There was a legendary cow with a large white stripe going down both sides of her shoulders that had escaped from a number of holdups over the years, and we had all heard of her. There was also a big steer, said to be eight years old, with beautifully shaped wide horns that had only been seen once or twice. Someone on the opposite side of the thicket hollered and said they thought the white-shouldered cow was in the bunch. I was on the downhill side of the thicket and thought maybe there could be a dozen critters bunched up inside, but I knew for sure the big steer was there because he was looking right at me

The cattle stopped for a few seconds and then bounced back and forth wanting to make a break, but each time someone turned them back to the center of the brush patch. Nothing was being said because words don't mean anything in a situation like this; you just have to react to your instincts and let the situation play itself out.

The big steer finally couldn't take it any longer and came toward the edge of the oaks leading several other cattle with him. Buck Smith and I jumped our horses in front of him and for a few seconds he stopped, and then finally he came. The hillside where we were was very steep, and there was no place bigger than 20 feet where there wasn't a tree of some kind, and in places they were only two feet apart. When the steer came out of the oaks he was hauling the mail and wasn't stopping except on the end of a rope. Buck and I jumped, trying to plug the hole, and managed to turn everything back except him. In that split second of eternity, we had to decide to pursue him or preserve the holdup, which contained an unknown number of cattle. We chose the holdup, and the steer was gone in a flash into the shadows of oak and pine trees. You could hear limbs breaking and rocks rolling for more than a few seconds as he

Big steer leavin' the hold up- *by Mike Capron*

---

crashed down off the mountain. He was the only one that got away. The truth is neither Buck nor I had a good lay at him at the time, and to catch him we would have had to follow him and do battle somewhere else where conditions were a little better. In the meantime the entire bunch might have gotten away. Forty-two years later I still see all 1600 pounds of him coming out of the oak thicket and wonder what might have been.

We managed to keep the rest of the cattle in the oak thicket from running off and eased them down the steep slope until we hit the bottom of the pass between the two mountains. There was an old road there and several places to establish a good holdup ground. We made several sashays out into the brush and managed to run several more cattle into our little holdup, which was now numbered close to twenty head of cattle including sucking calves. The old outlaw cow with the white shoulders was still there plus several full grown cows that we branded. We had been working in the area for several days now and had not driven anything off the mountain. Everything we had gathered so far had been roped and led off to a trap down by the Oaks and Willows. Today we would drive our sizeable holdup down the mountain, if possible. Whistle got out in the lead with Buck and Bob to his right, and Ed Evans and Joe Smith to his left. I was in the drags as we headed down the road toward home. As you went through the pass headed north, you turned west and began to descend down the north slope of Dairy Mountain. The trees and brush were thick, and the farther we went the steeper the mountain became, dropping off rapidly to our right. All of a sudden a three-year-old maverick cow busted out of the herd right behind Bob's horse and went sailing down the mountain in a dead run, and it was downhill and shady. Bob was riding a horse he had just traded for. He was a five-year-old that had always been gentle, but didn't know much. When the cow made her escape, Bob was gone after her in a flash going downhill in a run and in a second was out of sight. We held the cattle up thinking that Bob would return soon. For a few seconds we could hear rocks rolling and limbs bending or breaking, and then we heard a very loud sound not unlike a vehicle crashing into a large tree. It was quiet after that, and we paid attention to our cattle that required constant surveillance. After no more than ten minutes, Bob came riding back up the mountain, and when he got near enough to talk, Whistle commented, "She got away I reckon." To which Bob replied that, no, actually the cow was tied down about three hundred yards below us. His new horse had a very large triangular-shaped piece of hide lying over his nostrils and an equally large piece of bloody skull exposed that went from his eyeballs halfway down the bridge of his nose. He explained that when he got close enough to start swinging his rope his horse stampeded into the trunk of a large pinion pine

Whistle ropin' a yearlin' - *by Mike Capron*

---

tree and knocked himself out for a second. Evidently, he had never been roped on and the commencing of that event scared him. In spite of all that, Bob had got him up, and moving, and caught the cow anyway. After we got our herd penned down the trail several miles, Bob and Whistle went back up the side of the mountain and tied the cow to a tree.

On the last day we worked on the mountain, we split up near the place where the maverick cow ran out of the herd with Bob in pursuit. We were going downhill heading north toward Seep Dam. Whistle had two favorite horses, old Turdhead and another gelding about the same size named Whiskey. I got down the mountain before anyone else and stopped at the edge of the clearing that was going to be our holdup ground. Within a minute or two I heard a commotion a hundred yards west of where I was stopped, and in a moment a big fat dry cow appeared going fast and Whistle in hot pursuit; Bob was a few yards behind. When the cow reached the clearing at a high rate of speed Whistle roped her around the horns and dallied. Whistle always packed about 30 feet of rope with a braided horn knot in the end of it, but I never saw him tied to the horn, but he would dally on a slick horn. Whistle had jumped a cow that was by herself and a chase started immediately without having the time to cinch up properly, and the cow weighed around 1300 pounds. In a second or two the cow, who was roped slick around the horns, had jerked Whistle's saddle down on Whiskey's side while Whistle hollered, "Heel her, Bob! Heel her!" It is the only recollection I have of Whistle raising his voice. He did not let go until Bob had roped a hind leg and pulled the cow down, even though his 76-year-old head was dragging on the grass. Good ole' Whiskey just stood there acting like it was his idea to take care of the old man.

Through the years I have heard other men criticize Whistle and say he didn't know how to make a drive, or handle big herds of cattle, or that he didn't know how to manage a ranch. I do know that while I worked at the O RO the cattle were exceptionally gentle if you consider the rough brushy country they ran in. I remember the spring of 1971, we gathered about 35 unbranded cattle that were a year or older, most of them being yearlings; a very small number, considering the ranch was running 3500 cows. The only big wild steer on the ranch that I knew of was the one we saw on the side of Bear Mountain. The outfit was simple: we branded in the spring and shipped in the fall, and in between we broke a few colts to ride and packed a little salt. The ranch had about an 80 percent calf crop. There weren't any horror stories floating around Prescott in the saloons and feed stores about big bands of wild steers and unbranded cattle, that originated with deer hunters who hunted on the ranch after

O RO shipping day at Oaks and Willows Nov 1971, Photo courtesy of Roy Olson

Whistle was dead and gone. Sometimes less can be more - or so the saying goes. Perhaps that is true with ranch management. Whistle, Buck, Coley, and Ralph were old men I didn't appreciate enough. I wish I could walk down the screened-in porch of that nice bunkhouse at the Oaks and Willows and pass by Ralph's door. Through the haze of cigarette smoke illuminated by that one light bulb, I would stare at the one reading and the other sitting there contemplating a cow brute, and without knowing it, enjoying each other for a spell. I am a thief because, without them seeing me, I invaded their solitude and stole a picture that will be imbedded in my brain forever.

Mohon Camp circa 1965. Photo courtesy of Ada Heckethorn

೮೦೦೪

Raymond Holt

೮೦೦೪

I am not eccentric.
It's just that I am more alive than most people.
I am an unpopular electric eel set in a pond of catfish.
Rebecca McKinsey

R aymond Holt began life in northeastern Arizona, south
of Holbrook, around 1898, where his family had a
homestead somewhere in the vicinity of Snowflake or
Taylor. Among other things the family tried to make a living as
dryland farmers. In old age, when asked why their endeavors
as dryland farmers weren't successful, he would comment, "It
got to durn wet." Raymond had three brothers: Lige, Skillet,
and Buster; all of whom became cowboys. Raymond, Skillet,
and Buster worked hard and pooled their money and sent Lige
to college. When asked what Lige profited from his college
education, Raymond would say, "He never amounted to anymore
than a fair to middlin' bronc rider."

Raymond was about 5 feet 6 inches tall and never weighed
over 160 pounds; he was electric with energy, and did everything
with a do-or-die attitude. Adversity never depressed him.
Though never loud or obnoxious, he was far too opinionated
to be accused of being quiet. He loved excitement and wasn't
beyond causing a wreck just to feel adrenaline in his veins.

In 1932 Raymond was cooking for a large ranch owned

by some people named Nutter, which was on the Arizona strip north of the Grand Canyon. For some reason, he had angered a neighboring sheep rancher whose name was Woods. One account has Raymond traveling to St. George, Utah, to buy groceries for the wagon, and while in the store he had flirted with Woods's beautiful daughter. Mr. Woods, who was a Mormon,

Raymond Holt Remodeling the Cook Tent - *by Mike Capron*

didn't approve of a "nonbeliever" looking at the young girl, let alone making small talk with her; and he and Raymond ended up having words over the affair.

Several days later Raymond was back on the Nutter Ranch cooking at the wagon for the roundup crew. Around midday he was under the fly busy making bread on the top of the chuck box lid, which was let down making a counter top. Nearby a young boy named Logue Morris, who was 15 years old, was bringing in the horses for a noon change. The roundup crew was due to show up at meal time. Mr. Woods, the sheep rancher whom Raymond had encountered several days earlier, rode up. Logue Morris and Raymond both saw him approaching. Woods rode up real close to the wagon and without warning produced a 45. Colt revolver and started shooting at Raymond. At the first shot his horse reared up with him, causing his second and third shots to stray even farther than the first, all of which missed the cook whom he was aiming for. Raymond had a 38. Special revolver laying in a drawer of the chuck box, and with the first shot hit Woods in the abdomen; and he fell off his horse and gave up the fight.

Logue Morris saw the whole thing, being only a few feet away. He would later tell how, minutes after the shooting stopped, he had observed a can of evaporated milk with a bullet hole in it setting only a few inches away from the bread dough, and it still had milk dripping out of it. Woods was only wounded, and with the help of Logue's uncle, Perley, who was also working for the outfit, they loaded Woods in Perley Morris' car and hauled him to town and a doctor; and Woods made a full recovery.

Woods pressed charges saying Raymond had assaulted him; and although there was a great deal of evidence that Raymond had acted in self-defense, the charges stuck, and Raymond had to defend himself in court. To the natives who lived on the strip and in southern Utah, Raymond was a foreigner from south of the Ditch, and there was a huge faction that wanted to hang him. The trial was held in Kingman, Arizona, the county seat of Mohave County, and because of Logue Morris' testimony saying Woods had fired first and without warning, Raymond was acquitted.

In the late '30s or '40s, Raymond worked for the 3Vs north of Seligman. The 3Vs later became known as the Diamond A. There was a young cowboy also working on the 3Vs complaining about a bronc in his string who was bad about stampeding, and being in general difficult to control. The horse had probably been consuming loco weed as a side dish. Raymond, known for his endless energy and wild antics, decided to help the young pilgrim by instructing him how to survive when a young outlaw horse was giving you a first hand runaway experience. Raymond saddled up the bronc, and while the entire cowboy crew stood next to the wagon watching, he rode the cayuse, managing to keep him in control about 200 yards distance. He then turned

Raymond Holt; Cook and Horse Wrangler - *by Mike Capron*

---

him back toward the wagon, whipping him into an out-of-control stampede. Twenty yards or so away from the wagon there was an algerita bush about five feet high and full of the prickly and thorny leaves, which the plants possesses. Raymond guided the runaway near the algerita, and as the horse passed by he bailed off into the bush in a spectacular fashion. He then stood up and walked towards the wagon shaking his finger in the air and proclaiming, "You just jump off a runaway into a bush or tree, and it will break your fall, and you won't get killed that way!" While he brushed the limbs and thorns off himself, he asked the buttons if they wanted to try it. He didn't get any takers.

The cowboy crew was cutting two-year-old studs at Pica Camp 17 miles west of Seligman one day. Raymond decided, perhaps on a dare, that he would entertain himself by riding the stud colts. They would run the colts one at a time into a round corral, and then forefoot them, and tie them down to castrate them. Before they roped the colts, Raymond would stand

astraddle of the top rail on the fence and bail off onto the back of the loose horse. He did this several times providing a great deal of entertainment to everyone present. Finally, after jumping on several, a colt bucked him off and cracked a vertebra in his neck. This stopped his antics for the day, and he had to wear a neck brace for awhile, but otherwise the incident didn't change him much.

Raymond was cooking for the 3Vs wagon sometime around 1940, and they were short-handed. Kilo Pruitt was the wagon boss, and he needed to move a large herd of cattle and move camp the same day. While thinking out loud with Raymond within hearing distance, he was calculating how he could get the cattle and the camp moved with so little help. Raymond told him not to worry about a thing, saying he could move the wagon and the remuda by himself. Raymond had Kilo rope him a good broke horse, which he saddled and tied to the chuck box at the back of the wagon. While Kilo took the rest of the crew, including the man who usually served as horse wrangler, to gather and move the big herd of cattle, Raymond hitched up the team, and loaded the wagon, and took off toward the new campsite. After going several miles, Raymond stopped the wagon, and hobbled the team, and then mounted the saddle horse that had been following tied to the chuck box. He loped back to where they had been camped and gathered the remuda, driving the horses by the wagon and on past for several miles distance. He then loped back, tying the saddle horse to the back of the wagon again. He kept repeating this process several times until he reached the place Kilo had said he wanted to set up camp. When Kilo and his crew rode up late in the afternoon, camp was set up and the coffee was on, with the remuda grazing nearby.

In the 1940s and early '50s, Raymond worked as wagon cook for the well-respected cowboy and wagon boss Lopey Heller on the famous ZX Ranch in southeastern Oregon. The ZX was, and still is, one of the biggest ranches in the west, and because of its size and cattle numbers, cow work never ceased. Lopey Heller was famous for his steady head and even-tempered ability to handle a crew, as well as a herd of cows. Lopey, after much politicing, had appropriated enough money from the company to purchase a new cook tent: A comfort that everyone in the crew appreciated. One morning a member of the crew mounted a well-known outlaw horse not far from where the tent was set up with Raymond inside working. Raymond, when hearing the commotion, and not wanting to miss the action, grabbed a large butcher knife and sliced a large hole in the side of the new tent so he could stick his head out and watch the bronc ride. The tent flaps were tied shut because of the cold wind, and untying them would have used up valuable time. Raymond worked for Lopey ten years and, with the exception of that incident, they got along well.

Raymond went to work for the Babbitt Ranch north of Flagstaff around 1964. He would stay up on the mountain at Wild Bill Camp in the summer and down on the Little Colorado River in the winter. Raymond could get along with a crew, or by himself, it didn't matter to him. Like most people who tend to be happy all the time, he had the ability to see humor in small things. He would talk to himself, and probably had the ability to play the role of several people at once. But he was not crazy; in fact, he possessed a mind like a steel trap, and he observed everything. He could, and would, be as sarcastic and critical as an old scrooge with severe gout; especially, if he thought it was bothering you, but he was not hateful. He liked young people if he thought they were willing to take his advice. He was not a drinker, although he probably had some whiskey hidden for snakebites and other emergencies. Above all he was a company man, and his main focus in everything he did was to make a hand, preferably at full throttle.

One time he was gathering remnants off the forest in the Slate Lake Pasture on the CO Bar. He found an old Hereford bull on the west side of the highway and needed to cross him to the other side and drive him to Cedar Ranch five miles away. The horse he was riding had eaten loco weed several times in his life and wasn't exactly wired correctly. The bull refused to cross the pavement, so Raymond roped him with over 30 feet of nylon tied hard and fast to the saddle horn. The little loco horse either couldn't or wouldn't pull the bull. For awhile they were in a stalemate and then Raymond had an idea. With his horse facing the highway, he backed him up toward the bull's head, coiling up the slack in his tied rope as he did so. When he got four or five feet from the bull's head; the bull, who was mad anyway, would charge and stick a horn into the locoed horse's rear, who would in turn stampede straight ahead until he hit the end of the rope, jerking the bull forward several feet. Raymond repeated this process until he got the bull jerked all the way across the pavement. Raymond was 71 or 72 years old when he did this and considered it just another day on the job.

In January of 1975, Raymond came to Spider Web to talk to Bill Howell, the wagon boss, and told him he was going to retire. He had been staying at the River Camp, which was 15 miles to the east of Spider Web. "I just can't cut the mustard anymore, Bill," he complained. "I was shoeing a horse this morning and used 25 nails, bending one so bad I had to throw it away. Anybody that is that sorry doesn't have any business hanging around drawing wages." Bill talked him into staying until July 1 and cook for the wagon. He was as good a wagon cook as I ever knew and was very clean. He made excellent sourdough bread and pancakes.

One morning toward the end of June, a cowboy got bucked off and hurt pretty badly as we were trotting away from the Redland's horse corral. Pat Cain and his wife Faye were living at Redlands at the time. Pat asked Faye to fire up their big Buick car and haul the injured cowboy into the doctor in Flagstaff 90 miles away. Faye Cain was a real character in her own right and always had a twinkle in her eye. As we were loading the man into the backseat of the big Buick, Raymond stepped out of the bunkhouse and handed Faye a pint of whiskey that he had hidden somewhere among his personal belongings. "Thank you," Faye said, "I'm sure he'll need some pain killer on the way to town!"

"No, no!" Raymond replied loudly as the injured man groaned, "Hell with that sorry *#x/*x, the whiskey is for you; you're going to get tired of listening to him piss and moan, so you drink it!"

Old log barn at Cedar Ranch, circa 1965.

Grandstanding for the Photographer - *by Mike Capron*

ഇരു

Jep Stell

ഇരു

A miser grows rich by seeming poor,
An extravagant man grows poor by seeming rich.
William Shenstone

Jep Stell was born in Texas in the late 1890s, probably in 1899, somewhere in the vicinity of Uvalde. In the 1940s he migrated to Northern Arizona where he found work on the big ranches around Seligman. I know he worked on the Diamond A Ranch in the late '40s for a wealthy Californian. I heard him tell a story how the owner hired a professional photographer to come to Rose Well to take pictures. According to Jep, the Californio had the cowboy crew gather a large herd of cattle, and hold them up outside, and positioned the photographer where he could photograph him roping big cows that he cut out of the herd one at a time. Jep considered this to be phony grandstanding and heartily disapproved.

There were stories that Jep had, in earlier days, supplemented his income as a bartender and a professional gambler. He was not prone to talk a lot about his past and was most certainly not given to bragging, but several times he mentioned big card games he had been in. He loved to play poker still when I knew him in his mid 70s, especially five card stud. He considered seven card stud a child's game and beneath the dignity of a true gambler. He had a poker face and said very little as he played.

Jep, like so many of his generation, had a cultivated peculiarity. Being different wasn't something he was ashamed of. One could have almost wondered if being different had been a goal he had set his sights on when a young man; yet that was, in my opinion, not the case. He was whom he was, and didn't really care about any certain thing that might have been noticed by someone around him. He gambled, but he was as honest as any man I ever knew. He was quiet and yet, once in awhile, could come up with a one-liner that would leave a crew of men rolling on the ground with laughter, though I never heard him laugh out loud. He was good natured but he didn't put up with anybody messing with him.

Once when he first came to Arizona, he was working at the O RO Ranch south of Seligman. He, along with several men, was shoeing the remuda. Jep was shoeing a mule who was giving him a considerable amount of trouble. Finally Jep's patience ran out, and he began delivering a few substantial blows to the mule's body, using a rasp for a club. Oscar Coleman, the manager, happened to drive up in a pickup and witnessed the fight between Jep and the mule. Oscar, who liked to play the big shot, asked Jep in the most authoritative voice he could muster, "What are you doing to that mule, Jep?"

Jep replied, "Hell, Oscar, any dumb */#*!# could tell I'm beating the hell out of a mule!" Jep wasn't impressed with or afraid of Oscar Coleman.

For a number of years Jep worked for Leland Larson when Leland managed the Diamond A. There was at that time a cow camp on the far north end of the ranch near the boundary of the Supai Indian Reservation and the edge of the Grand Canyon. This particular camp was called Bishop. There is nothing left there today but remains of the camp house foundation. Jep was staying there by himself one winter. One bitter cold morning Jep sat at the kitchen table drinking coffee. Suddenly there appeared five Supai Indians mounted on horses, and they lined up side by side outside the kitchen window. Jep sat at his chair and stared at them, and they stayed mounted and stared back with typical Indian stoicism. Knocking on a door and requesting an audience

Jep Stell Overhauling a Mule - *by Mike Capron*

---

is not an Indian trait. This game of chicken to see who could act more outlandish went on for sometime. Finally the five Indians got the best of him, and Jep stepped out onto the porch and exclaimed, "What the hell's wrong with you sorry */#*/#!? Do you think I'm crazy?" The five Indians, who remained silent, all responded in orchestrated unison by nodding their heads up and down in the affirmative. Then they turned and rode off.

In 1952 Jep bought himself a new Cadillac car which he drove until I knew him 23 years later. Old Route 66 went through the middle of the small town of Ashfork, Arizona: the highway making up the two main thoroughfares, a westbound two-laned street, and one block to the south, a two-lane eastbound street.

Before I-40 was built bypassing the town, these streets were very busy at all times. One day Jep pulled out of the post office parking lot and headed west on the busy eastbound section of Route 66. An old lady witnessed this deliberate infraction as she passed by on the sidewalk. "Old man, old man, you're going the wrong way!" She exclaimed, waving her arms in the air trying to get his attention.

Jep, who chewed Tinsley's plug tobacco and was famous for his expertise as a spitter, hung his head out the window and shouted back, "Old woman, I'm only going two blocks!" After answering, he deposited a particularly large load of Tinsley juice on the pavement and the side of the Cadillac, putting an exclamation point on his "I don't care" rebuttal.

In 1969 Jep showed up in Flagstaff and found his way to the Babbitt Ranch office which was on the second floor of the old Babbitt building across the street from the Monte Vista Hotel. Jep was seeking instructions on how to get an interview with John Babbitt, or Bill Howell, the wagon boss and manager. Jep had been put on hold by someone in the office and stood silently waiting for some knowledgeable person to assist him, when in walked Raymond Holt, who was about the same age, probably 71 or 72. Raymond had been working for Babbitts for six years and was in the office to get his mail and a paycheck. The two knew each other by reputation but had never worked together. Both men were skeptical of anyone who hadn't proven their worth in some personal way, and like a couple old coyotes were wary to a fault. Jep stood in silence like Kawliga the wooden Indian as Raymond, who was at least a foot shorter but much more caustic of tongue, observed him from a distance, mentally calculating his worth as a man. "Kinda' old to be workin' for an outfit like this aren't you?" Raymond commented dryly.

"Still like to eat!" replied Jep, as he stared straight ahead refusing to honor Raymond with a look in the eye. Jep got the job.

Bill Howell put Jep in a cow camp known as the Tubs on the CO Bar Ranch and for the next five years the Tubs Camp was Jep's responsibility. He did not work with the cowboy crew except when the crew was camped with him at the Tubs and was rounding up in the country he took care of. Like most old bachelor cowboys, Jep knew how to cook, and the first fall Jep worked for the outfit he filled in as cook for a few days until a steady cook could be found. The first morning he cooked, he was frying eggs two at a time as the men stood in line waiting. He would ask each man, "How do you like your eggs?" as he cracked a couple into the frying pan. Johnny Babbitt and Tim Prosser, who were about 19 years old, both replied they liked their eggs any old way. "Oh! Any old way." Jep replied when they answered his query. The eggs came out of the pan a little on the raw side. The next morning he asked the same question and Tim and Johnny gave the same answer. The eggs were a little rawer. Finally, about the third day, Jep was serving the boys raw eggs, and Tim gave in and commented how he liked his cooked a little more, and Jep produced two of the most perfectly cooked eggs anyone had ever seen. Johnny Babbitt never gave in and ate raw eggs for about ten days.

Around 1951, or so, Jep had a sort of epiphany and realized he had gambled and wasted his money to the point of having nothing. He decided to start saving so he would have a nest egg for his old age. He bought the new Cadillac in 1952 and thereafter saved every penny he could, and by the time I met him he claimed to have money in four banks. The FDIC, at that time, would insure savings up to $20,000 in any one bank, so it was estimated he had over $60,000 in savings.

I first met Jep in 1974 when I went to work for Babbitts. The first time I saw him, he was wearing a pair of lime green coveralls that he had bought at K-Mart because they were cheap. He had cut the bib off the front of the coveralls and folded the newly cut edge over and used brass rivets instead of thread to bind up the frayed edge. It was a particularly cold, windy day, and he had on a yellow slicker with a piggin' string tied around his waist, using the slicker as a windbreak. He would buy the best Stetson hat money could buy and would wear it in one position until the spot on the brim on the right side, where he tugged at it with his hand, began to break. He would then begin wearing it about 90 degrees to the right, pulling on a different spot to keep it on. Each time the hat would become worn to his satisfaction at that position, he would rotate it another 90 degrees until finally the hat made the full circle. The process would take several years. He owned a real good pair of high-heeled Blucher boots and wore them every day. He had driven hobnails in the heels to make them last longer. He rode an old Cogshell saddle that had been made for him around 1950 before he quit spending money. When I first met him he had just paid a good saddle maker named Bob McCray to recover it. He owned one good bridle bit made by Ed Blanchard and a pair of long-shanked Crockett spurs that were probably made in the 1920s. A heavy pair of bat wing chaps rounded out his outfit. He stood six foot five inches and wasn't packing any fat. He was old but didn't ask any favors or expect to get any.

His miserly ways had made him famous. He would venture into Flagstaff once a month to get groceries and the mail. His one luxury was a case of Olympia beer, which he kept under his bed. Each night he would allow himself a beer. His groceries were furnished by the company, but he was stingy with them also; he would hide a box of cookies in a special place in the cupboard eating one or two a day. The man who got into his cookie stash without asking would get a cussing for sure. One time Harvey Howell stopped by the Tubs Camp in a company pickup that had a pinhole leak in the gas tank. Jep wasn't home, so without asking, Harvey went inside the house and got a bar of soap out of the shower, thinking he could temporarily plug the leak with soap, and on his way out of the house, Harvey lifted two of Jep's cookies to snack on. Jep informed Bill Howell that there were thieves in the country who were stealing soap and cookies. Most of the time he was in camp by himself, so it didn't matter.

One time the wagon was camped at the Tubs, and when this happened a couple times a year, the crew basically moved in with him. One evening after supper, four or five of us were sitting at the kitchen table playing penny ante poker. Jep was particularly fond of this activity and was enjoying himself immensely. As always he was chewing Tinsley's and every so often would lift a three pound coffee can and spit in it. While someone else was dealing, he got up and opened a cupboard door that held some of his personal camp groceries. He took down a can of peaches and opened them. He got in a drawer and got himself a large tablespoon and returned to the card game eating peaches straight out of the can while simultaneously chewing Tinsley's. After consuming about half the can, he looked up as if startled and proclaimed loudly, "I'm sorry, boys, you want some peaches?" holding the can towards us while talking. Remnants of mixed peach and tobacco juice were visible on the spoon and the can.

"No thanks, Jep," we all replied in unison.

Jep had a reputation of being difficult to get along with according to some old-timers, but I thought he was a man to respect in spite of his numerous oddities. I never heard him raise his voice toward anyone. He never complained and did not talk bad about the outfit or the man he was working for.

As the Tubs camp man, he was responsible for over two hundred-plus square miles of country. I never saw or heard of him having the use of a ranch truck. It was a full 15 miles from the Tubs to the West Knobs fence, and he more than once rode the distance and moved cattle away from a drying up dirt tank or performed some other duty that was required of him. It is at least 10 miles from the Tubs to Lockwood where the CO Bar bulls were kept in the winter. Jep would ride there and back to cut ice in the wintertime, many times in deep snow and below zero temperatures. I never heard a single story about Jep allowing an animal to die of thirst at a dried up tank or drown, breaking through the ice in winter because of his negligence. There was always a tired looking horse and a pile of worn-out horse shoes near the Tubs saddle house. Possibly the most profound testament to his worth as an employee was, I have no recollection of Bill Howell saying anything bad about him. He was treated with respect.

Sometime in April of 1975, I was down in the horse corral at Spider Web, the CO Bar headquarters. I noticed Jep's 1952 Cadillac pull up in front of Bill Howell's house, which was about six hundred yards distance. I had never seen Jep at Spider

Web before and wondered what prompted this unusual event. I continued working with a young horse while the Cadillac remained parked for about 30 minutes, and then I saw Jep reenter the big car and head my way. He pulled up and stopped outside the corral gate, and when he shut the engine off he stepped out, and after coming through a corral gate he walked toward me. He was dressed in an old blue pinstriped suit that was probably 35 years old. He had a thin black ribbon tied in a bow around the collar of an old white shirt. He had on a good silver belly Stetson hat, and his famous hobnailed Blucher boots that had been polished.

I was inside another corral busying myself with a colt that I was breaking. I paused and walked over to the fence, and we shook hands, him being on one side of the fence and me being on the other. "I come to say good bye." He said in a matter-of-fact tone. I inquired as to the reason of our apparent parting. He told me that it was time for him to retire, slightly inferring that he felt incapable of doing his job as well as he should. He told me that he had an old sister down in Uvalde that he could go and live with. We stood there for a few moments not saying much. He leaned forward resting his elbows on a fence rail, and stared through the fence at the colt, and seemed for a moment to be content to just be there not saying anything. Directly he straightened up, and he nodded at me and turned around and began walking toward his car. He took a couple steps and then turned and said, "You're a good hand." And with that, he stepped into the Cadillac and left in a cloud of dust. I never saw him again. It was a compliment I will never forget.

Tubs camp house CO Bar Ranch.

Wonder How Many Calves It Took To Pay For That Little Darling - *by Mike Capron*

ഇാൽ

A Cowboy Job Interview

ഇാൽ

The employer generally gets the employee he deserves.
J. Paul Getty

I first heard about the job from old Bill who had been running the outfit for a dozen or so years. Bill had been well paid, and being prudent in his investments had accumulated enough wealth to retire, an event he was looking forward to. He had notified several cowboys around the country who, in his estimation, were capable of taking his place. For some reason unbeknownst to me, I was among that bunch, and an interview had been arranged.

The owner of the outfit had built himself a mansion on a rocky promontory overlooking a spring that produced several hundred gallons of water a minute. The real headquarters of this 1000 cow outfit lay a dozen miles north, and beings the vast supply of water was not used for anything more than watering a few cows, I was confused why a man would build a home so far from the center of all the cow work. Perhaps he liked the view, and perhaps cow work was the farthest thing from his mind.

We were supposed to arrive at 10:00 a.m., which would provide time to talk business, and then our prospective employer would serve lunch. We were ushered into the interior of the well-appointed home that boasted of brass light fixtures and a wood stove imported from England. The ranch owner was a wealthy professional who had been introduced into the cow business through inheritance. She, like the brass light fixtures and stove, was an English import and was cool but friendly. He was cool.

While my wife and the lady of the house visited and talked of preparing the midday meal, the doctor and I retired to the parlor to talk business. I was prepared to give evidence of all my accomplishments as a cowboy, cowman, and all-around managerial candidate. He, with the appearance of one whose veins contained ice water, gazed at me for some moments without speaking. I held my peace and at last he spoke, "Have you ever overhauled a diesel engine?"

I had been prepared to tell him of the broncs I had busted and the wild cows I had roped. I could brag about working for the likes of Whistles Mills, John Andrews, Jim Miller, and Bill Howell. I had watched the sun rise over the top of Mount Hope and go down on the Painted Desert, but the plain truth was, no, I had never overhauled a diesel engine! For two hours I was grilled repeatedly about engines, the square root of seventeen, and my ability to communicate with government bureaucracies like the U. S. Forest Service and the NRCS. At no time did a question arise about my knowledge of gathering cattle, working cattle, the cattle industry as a whole, or the cow market in particular. There was no mention of cattle pedigrees, heterosis, estrus, or the available protein and vitamin A in Northern Arizona forbs during a typical January at 6000 feet elevation.

Nobody who owned a hospital would hire a cat skinner to manage it. I couldn't help but wonder why a rancher would hire a mechanic to run the ranch. I was becoming apprehensive about my test score; in other words, I knew I was failing.

Finally, the ladies announced that lunch was ready. Knowing the well-appointed kitchen had among other necessities an imported wood stove, I envisioned a feast: big fluffy baking powder biscuits with gravy along side, a big dose of pounded, floured and fried round steak came to my mind, and then maybe some peach cobbler cooked in the oven of the famous English stove with some hot black cowboy coffee to wash it all down.

We entered the dining area, which was cold, and I noticed

a decorative flower pot on the English stove. No fire there. And then I caught my first glimpse of the table, four china plates and four glasses of water. In the middle of the table was a platter displaying slabs of some cut of meat that was more gristle than muscle. The meat was cold, which I learned is what cold cuts are supposed to be. There was a jar of Best Foods mayonnaise and another plate that held a quantity of sliced tomatoes. To round all this out was a stack of sliced bread which rested on another vessel of imported china. The bread was Holsum, as in Holsum brand. I saw the plastic wrapper it came in resting on the kitchen counter. I was so ignorant of modern ranch management practices I didn't know tasteless bread like Holsum was allowed on cow outfits.

We sat down and I was careful to not rest my elbows on the table. Food was passed around and I took a portion of that which was available. I was patient and in time observed what our hosts intended to do with their victuals, and as a result of my craftiness, I began making a sandwich as if I knew what I was doing. I applied a great deal of mayonnaise which I figured would be the only ingredient containing that quality known as taste. I also applied several slices of tomato on top of the slab of cold rare meat which, being quite large, hung over the edge of the china. Before making a lid with a second slice of Holsum, I considered putting some salt and pepper on top of the central ingredients. But when I considered the appearance of the shakers, which looked like Fabergé eggs, I knew that would be hopeless. The implements containing these spices were of the type that have holes so small that no kernel of pepper or salt can escape. I thought about taking the lid off but realized that would be inappropriate.

What happened next will forever be branded into the inner sanctums of my ego, paralyzing my confidence, and laying waste my ability to calculate the future: I lifted the sandwich with its slab of gristle and took a large bite. I instantly realized my forty-year-old incisors would not cut through and allow me to separate that which was in from that which was out. I hesitated, knowing it wasn't the time to be hasty. I glanced around and could tell everyone was trying to ignore me. I would act decisively biting down with all my strength, and then with one great tearing motion would separate that portion of slab that was in my mouth.

Swiftness, as well as strength, would be needed, and so with one great motion I pulled downward with two hands and bit solidly into the cold cut. Trying to be a gentleman, I had, upon entering the house several hours earlier, deposited my sombrero on a hat rack by the door. I so missed it at this point in time because, being unable to hide behind the wide brim, I could tell everyone was now staring at me. My hands held two slices of Holsum, which were well lubricated with an ample supply of Best Foods mayonnaise and several slices of tomato. A large slab of beef hung downward out of my mouth, looking a great deal like a Peterbuilt mud flap that had been riveted to my lower lip.

In a moment of time I caught a brief sparkle originating from the imported brass light fixtures and reflected on the tomato juice amidst the Holsum my hands held. It was like a revelation, or epiphany of sorts, and suddenly I knew that I was not going to get the job.

Cowboy skills unrelated to rebuilding a diesel engine. Photo by Vicki Grant.

Showing the Boys How To Do It - *by Mike Capron*

ക്രൗ
Hard Times, Good Times
ക്രൗ

He is now rising from affluence to poverty.
Mark Twain

A good many old-timers that I knew and worked with when I was starting out were from the Hot Springs, New Mexico, area. Today, Hot Springs goes by the name of Truth or Consequences, but to the old cowboys I knew, it was Hot Springs. Buck Smith, Raymond Scott, Jack George and Burley and Elmer McDonald were all from that general area, as was the famous cowboy and rodeo producer, Johnny Mullins. Bob Burris, who is one of the best men I've ever known or worked for, was raised up the river a spell from Hot Springs, and so was his brother-in-law, Jim Lowrance, who managed the Diamond A Ranch at Seligman when I first worked there in 1972.

Buck Smith was raised on a small ranch near Engel, east of Hot Springs, and would tell me stories of growing up in the land of Jornado del Muerto and the northern sphere of the Chihuahua Desert. The landscape in this area has always been shaped by the never too distant memories of hot winds and impending drought. When an occasional wet winter brings on a good spring, noxious weeds may kill more cattle than the drought a rancher had to live through a year before. The people who eked out a living raising livestock in this part of the world have always been some of the toughest that ever lived. Poverty was a noticeable commodity by the standards of the ranch people in this part of New Mexico in the first half of the twentieth century. The ever present harsh elements punctuated by the economic ravages of the Great Depression made just getting by a common denominator among men.

Buck told me one day he and his father rode horseback a good distance from their ranch to see some people with whom his dad had some business to discuss. Buck was a teenage boy and had never been to these people's ranch and apparently neither had his father. Their ranch was isolated and a good ways distance to the nearest neighbor. The two of them rode up to the house and Buck's father dismounted and knocked on the door expecting the people to be there. Finding no one home they remounted their horses and started to ride off when they noticed an odd looking pen. Not realizing they were being nosey, they rode over to the pen that was, in fact, more like a cage. It was built out of woven page or sheep wire, and there was the same type of wire on the ground and overhead enabling the pen to incarcerate anything larger than a small rabbit. On one end of the cage was a makeshift shelter made out of a few boards and corrugated tin. Inside the cell was a teenage girl, who stood staring at them as they rode up, and when they got close she ran and hid in the shelter, peeking out to look at them occasionally. There was a bucket of water tied to the side of the cage. They tried to communicate but soon realized she was severely retarded, and her family kept her locked up to prevent her from running away when they were gone. In Buck's telling of the story, there was no hint of accusation of cruelty or parental neglect. The people simply did not have the financial means to deal with the situation in a different manner. There was no government agency or funding either suggesting or forcing a different course of action; you simply got by the best way you could.

When Buck left home he started cowboying around on the bigger ranches and acquired a reputation as a bronc rider. He rode broncs at rodeos in Hot Springs and other nearby towns that were produced by Johnny Mullins whom he worked with at the O RO Ranch north of Prescott when the two were old men. The great test of riding skill in vogue at the rodeos where

Leland Larson. Photo courtesy Nellie McDonald

he competed was to ride with a silver dollar between the sole of your boot and the stirrup; a feat he was successful at. There was a famous outlaw mule that someone hauled around to the rodeos,

Left to right Janice, Carolyn, Allene, Nellie, and JoAnn McDonald. Photo courtesy Nellie McDonald.

and they would challenge any comers to ride him for a 50 dollar prize. Buck said the only time he saw the mule successfully ridden was by a local teenage girl with long yellow braids. Buck left home and roamed around southern New Mexico for several

Burley McDonald. Photo courtesy Nellie McDonald.

Above: Tom Dolan and Leland Larson. Photo courtesy Jim Dolan

Early Diamond A Cowboys: John Mow, Unkown, Jim Gibson, Decan Sannich, Raymond Scott, Leland Larson, Walter Slater, Don Hinnan, Unknown, Unknown, Ed Brown, Jack Holloway, Elmer McDonald, Ernst Baty, Tom Dolan, Bob Ernest, Hoffman Camp, Seligman, Ariz. Photo courtesy Jim Dolan.

Janice, Allene, JoAnn, Carolyn, and Elmer McDonald. Photo courtesy of Nellie McDonald

years without seeing his folks. When he finally got lonesome for a visit, he showed back up at the ranch wearing a new black Stetson hat with a braided horsehair hatband. His father told him to get rid of the black hat and horsehair hatband or get off the outfit because outlaws dressed like that. Buck said he wore silver belly hats the rest of his life.

The biggest cow outfit between Hot Springs and Alamogordo was the famous Armendaris Ranch with landholdings totaling 380 thousand acres. The ranch was named after Pedro Armendaris, a lieutenant in the Spanish Royal Army, who was born in 1782. In a book written by George Anderson in 1907, the Armendaris is said to be owned by Victorio Land and Cattle Company whose head office was in Deming. Victorio Land and Cattle Company also owned the large Gray Ranch south of Animas. Anderson's book states that Victorio was owned by Kern County Land Company of Bakersfield, California, which also owned at different times numerous large ranches in several states, including several in the Bakersfield area: the famous Z X Ranch in Oregon, the little Boquillas in Cochise County, Arizona, and the Big Boquillas at Seligman, which was and still is Arizona's largest ranch. Kern County Land Company did not acquire the Seligman ranch until 1949, and before that time that ranch was known as the 3Vs. All the old men I mentioned in the first part of this chapter worked at the Armendaris when they were young men; Victorio Land and Cattle Company, and Boquillas Cattle Company were at the start subsidiaries of Kern County Land Company and the ranches in Arizona and New Mexico used the Diamond A brand on the thousands of cattle they ran on the various ranches. I've known many old-timers who worked for "the Company," as they would call it, most of their lives. If you questioned them about the specifics of the company they might say it was Victorio Land and Cattle Company, or the Boquillas Cattle Company, or Kern County Company, or they might simply say the Diamond A; but whatever the name the paycheck had on it, to them it was "the Company." Actually, to be specific, Victorio was the name of all the New Mexico ranches and the Arizona ranches were Boquillas Cattle Company, all of which were part of Kern County Land and Cattle Company.

Many old-timers worked for the Company on several different ranches in several states. Buck Smith knew Leland Larson when they were young and working on the Armendaris

Ranch whose headquarters was at Engle, east of Hot Springs. Leland migrated from there to the Gray Ranch south of Animas and Hatchita in Hidalgo County, and finally Leland moved to Seligman to manage the Big Boquillas when the Company bought the outfit in 1949. For a period of several years, Leland was in charge of all the Company's ranches in Arizona, and New Mexico, as well as the Z X Ranch in Oregon.

Buck Smith told me a story, when I worked for him at the O RO Ranch north of Prescott, that the first time he saw Burley McDonald was at the Armendaris Ranch. Burley came riding into the Armendaris on a horse that had seen better days, and according to Buck he was riding one of the most wore out looking saddles he had ever seen, with an oxbow stirrup on one side, and a flat bottom Visalia on the other. He was wearing lace up brogan shoes and a worn out pair of bib overalls. Burley and his brother Elmer were orphans and didn't exactly have an easy start, but regardless of looks, he found a job on the Armendaris and worked for the Company most of his life. When I first worked on the Big Boquillas at Seligman in 1972, Burley was the wagon boss on the upper wagon, and Mike Landis ran the lower wagon. Burley had an exceptional reputation as a cowman and cowboy and was famous for his photographic memory of livestock. He was very well liked by the men who worked for him

Burley's younger brother Elmer was a good friend of mine, as is his wonderful wife Nellie. Elmer spent a big part of his childhood in an orphanage. He was born in Tularosa in 1926, became an orphan, and was put in the orphanage when a baby. When he was 10 years old, an older sister came and took him to a small ranch in the Santa Andreas Mountains, east of Alamagordo, where she and her husband lived. The Depression was still raging, and Elmer's sister and brother-in-law, like most folks in the area, were just getting by. They had goats and Elmer became an expert goat herder and learned to use a sling, of the same type David used to kill Goliath, to ward off predators and to prod his herd with. When he was working one day, a horse fell over backwards with him and knocked a lot of his teeth out. This created problems for him for years, until as an adult he was able

Elmer and Nellie's: Everything You Need Is Right
Here On This Ranch - *by Mike Capron*

---

to afford some false teeth.

Nellie, whose maiden name was Johnson, was living on
the Armendaris Ranch where her father, Robert, was a camp
man. She had an uncle named Joey Gordon who was also an
Armendaris cowboy. Elmer came riding up to her dad's camp on
the Armendaris one day, and they met for the first time, and not
too long afterward they married.

Elmer and Nellie worked and lived on the Armendaris, and
after being married several years they moved to the Gray Ranch,
and stayed at the FitzPatrick, and later the Adobes. They did
a short stint on the Ladder Ranch, northwest of Hot Springs,
but migrated to the Boquillas at Seligman several years after the
Company bought the outfit in 1949 and sent Leland Larson to
Arizona to run it.

They left the Diamond A for several years and worked for Frank Banks on the Babbitt Ranch, and Elmer worked on a ranch near Beowawe, Nevada, for a spell, but most of their lives they worked for the Company; most of that time at the Boquillas north of Seligman. On one of their trips from New Mexico to Northern Arizona, they drove through Phoenix in an old 1940 Chevy car. Elmer had never been to a big city and had never seen an electric stoplight. He kept running red lights not realizing what they meant. Finally he got stopped behind some cars that were waiting for the light to turn green, and he figured it out.

When Elmer and Nellie first moved to Seligman to go work for Leland, they were moved into a cow camp at Red Lake, which by the road was close to forty miles north of town. It was late winter, and cold, and as soon as they got what little they owned unloaded someone came by and picked Elmer up and hauled him to the wagon, which was camped many miles away. Nellie didn't see him for at least a month. The house at Red Lake was nothing but a two-room shack, with no insulation or indoor plumbing of any kind. Their only heat was a small wood stove that also served as the cook stove. They were miles from nowhere, and Nellie didn't have a clue where somewhere else was, if she wanted to go there. She barely knew how to drive. On top of all that, she had four little girls, the oldest of which was five years old.

After staying a few months at Red Lake, Leland moved Elmer and Nellie to Supai, another twenty miles to the north. Nellie thought Supai was uptown because someone had built a cowboy refrigerator, which was a wooden box sticking out of a window that had a shelf or two in it. The sides might have holes in them or chicken wire, and you wrapped gunnysacks around the outside, that if kept wet would create a cooling effect for any food you might put inside the box.

Nellie spent her entire life in cow camps such as Supai, Red Lake, or Camp Five, which is where they lived when I first met them in 1972. She didn't want to be anywhere else. She and Elmer raised four beautiful daughters, all of whom grew up helping their dad punch cows one minute and their mom in the house the next. Nellie is one of the best cooks I ever ate after, as the saying goes. JoAnn, the youngest, married one of my best friends and I've eaten lots of her cooking as well as Nellie's. They both make gravy that is as smooth as honey. They can fry an egg so perfect it has absolutely no lace around the edge. What's so impressive about frying an egg? Perhaps nothing, until you think of all the people who can't do it right.

When Elmer and Nellie moved to Arizona, cowboys were making seventy dollars a month; your house had no electricity, you had no plumbing, and no guaranteed retirement. Elmer's oldest girl, Allene, told me that when she grew up, she told her mom one day that when she was five years old and living at Red Lake and Supai she thought they were rich. Nellie replied, "What in the world made you think we were rich?" Allene said that they got to live out there with all the beautiful scenery, and all the people that came to visit were interesting. All the poor people had to live in those ugly towns, so she figured they were rich.

Superman Beddin' Tom Down - *by Mike Capron*

Two Bad Days

ဆာ

If you think your teacher is tough, wait till you get a boss.
He doesn't have tenure.
Bill Gates

S ometimes things get out of control because you've let
them get that way, and sometimes they get out of control
because of conditions that are out of your control. I'll give
you an example.

In the spring of 1993, I was running the wagon on the
Diamond A Ranch north of Seligman, Arizona. We were
gathering the Cataract Plains on the north end of the ranch and
throwing the cattle south towards Rose Well where we would
brand the calves and turn the cows out to the south on summer
range. It was a slow process for a crew of about 15 cowboys that
took about three months to accomplish.

Around the first of May, we moved camp, from Camp
Number Five, south to a place known as Hazen Hole. There is
nothing at Hazen Hole except a stock pond, which in Arizona
is called a dirt tank; a water trough on a pipeline that originates
from Rose Well about 10 miles away; a barbwire corral, and a
small horse pasture. We got moved in the afternoon, set up the
cook tent and our teepees, and caught horses to ride the next
morning, which we kept in the barbwire pen. We ate supper that
our cook Floyd Martin prepared and settled in for the night.

The next morning we ate breakfast about an hour before first light, and then caught and saddled our horses, and took off at a lope and a trot, and headed straight west toward the backside of the Broken Axle pasture 10 miles away. Somewhere three or four miles north of the southeast corner of Broken Axle, I split the crew up. I took about half the men south, and Pat Prosser, who was my jigger boss, took the rest of the crew north, and we began making a drive back toward Hazen Hole where we planned to throw the cattle we gathered through a gate into a pasture called Midway.

One of the men Pat had with him on his side of the drive was his son Barney who was 18 or 19 years old. Barney was like all the other Prossers I've known, being an exceptional young cowboy who was well liked by everyone in the crew.

There were lots of cattle running in that country, and by the time we got halfway back to Hazen Hole we had perhaps five or six hundred cows strung out and moving in front of us. When we got about two miles from camp and the gate, which was our destination, I could look to the north and see numerous bunches of cattle coming down the slopes and headed in the right direction. Everything seemed to be going smoothly, when all of a sudden I saw a man riding a dark-colored horse racing toward camp in a dead run. He was two or three miles away, but I could see he was pickin' 'em up and setting 'em down, so to speak, and moving fast. It was too far to tell, but from the color of the horse and the direction he was coming from, I thought it must be Pat Prosser. Camp was out of sight behind a small hill so I couldn't tell what was going on, but within a few minutes after the horse disappeared in that direction, my Dodge pickup came from behind the hill and headed back north, and whoever was driving was doing so at a much higher rate of speed than I approved of, and the dust was rolling. I wondered to myself "What in the world is going on."

About an hour later, as I was within a quarter mile of the gate, a helicopter appeared on the horizon and then seemed to be landing three or four miles off to the north-northeast. Some other cowboys, who were close to me on drive, started showing up, and one of them brought word that Barney was hurt real bad, and they were loading him on a helicopter ambulance. Everyone had an opinion: his horse had stepped in a prairie dog hole and turned over with him; or, he had got bucked off and kicked; one said he had an epileptic seizure, although he had no history of having epilepsy; one of the men closest to Barney on the drive came running into camp crying and proclaimed that Barney was dying for sure.

Finally, after another hour, Pat drove back into camp, in my truck, a few moments after we all saw the helicopter take off and fly toward Flagstaff 100 miles away. Pat, understandably, was in a hurry, but explained to me that Barney was the last man he had dropped off, and things went smoothly for several hours. Pat had loped around a bunch of cattle and turned them toward Barney, who was hot on his heels flanking for him. Pat then saw another bunch a quarter mile away headed the wrong direction and took off in a lope to turn them. In doing so, he went over a hill and out of sight of Barney. Pat got the cattle turned back to the south and into the drive and was able to slow down a few moments, thinking that Barney would catch up with him shortly. After riding along for awhile, and Barney having not showed up, Pat turned and went back toward where they had last seen each other, thinking perhaps Barney needed help turning some cattle.

The cowboy Pat had dropped off before Barney was Randy Rutledge. Within several minutes of Pat leaving Barney and running to turn those cows into the drive, Randy topped a ridge and looked several hundred yards ahead of him and saw what looked like a man sitting on the ground with his hat off and his horse standing close by. At first he didn't think much of the situation and just eased that direction, but the closer he got the more out of the ordinary things looked. He kicked his horse into a lope, and when he reached the sitting man, he saw that it was Barney, and he had a long and deep cut across one side of his forehead. The wound was not bleeding real bad, but looked quite serious. Randy jumped off and asked Barney if he was alright and what had happened. Barney didn't reply, as he simply stared straight ahead, seemingly conscious, but unable to think or communicate.

Within another minute or two John McGrew showed up, and then suddenly Barney's eyes rolled back in his head, and he went into convulsions. The two cowboys were unsure what to do, and then Barney appeared to stop breathing. As they began administering CPR trying to revive him, Pat rode up, having doubled back to check on Barney when he hadn't caught up to him.

Randy and John told Pat that Barney was in pretty bad shape, and Pat whipped his horse into a dead run heading for camp to get my pickup, which had a two-way radio. As soon as he was in the truck he radioed the ranch manager, who in turn requested that a helicopter be sent to pick up the injured cowboy. Almost at once a helicopter took off from the Flagstaff hospital 100 miles to the southeast.

No one has ever figured out what exactly happened to Barney, but the best guess is his horse for some reason fell with him, and at sometime during the wreck he received a severe blow to his head. It took around two hours from when the wreck started until the helicopter landed and loaded him, taking him to the hospital. His father, Pat, came back to camp and loaded up in another company pickup that was his and headed south to Pica Camp where he lived, which was about 45 miles distance, with plans to go on to Flagstaff to be with his son.

The mood was pretty blue around the wagon as we ate lunch and listened to Randy and John relate what little they knew about the wreck that no one had witnessed. In their opinions, Barney had died three times, as he completely quit breathing while he lay unconscious waiting for the helicopter. Each time they pumped on his chest, trying to revive him, and then he would start breathing again.

Life goes on and staying busy is pretty good therapy when you're worried about a friend, so we caught ourselves a fresh horse and saddled up, figuring to gather some more cows. We headed our horses out the corral gate and traveled about a hundred yards when a sorrel horse named Superman started bucking with Tom Reeder. Tom was a Texas cowboy and about 52 years old. He and I had worked together for several years on the Babbitt Ranch, which bordered the Diamond A to the east. Tom worked for me at the Diamond A for a couple of years and was a very good cowboy and friend, but he couldn't ride a stick horse if it started bucking. Within two or three jumps Tom was on the ground and not getting up very fast.

Somebody ran and caught Superman, and I rode over to Tom and inquired about his health. He was up but listing to the left pretty bad, holding his left arm, and his glasses were resting

Pat Riding For Help - *by Mike Capron*

crooked on his nose. Tom stuttered real bad and was having a hard time communicating, so we all pulled up and waited for him to get his air and figure out if he was going to live or die. Sometimes it's best to let the injured assess the situation, so we waited.

I had known Tom for years and I liked him. He wasn't a great bronc rider, or a flashy roper, and not one to get a lot of attention from the photographers or the girls; but he was a good solid cowboy. His real expertise was his knowledge of cattle. If you had a large roundup throwed together, say 500 or a 1000 cows, and needed a lot of cutting or sorting done before sundown, he was a good man to have helping you. He knew what he was looking at when he looked at a cow. He was very loyal to me when he worked for me, and I appreciated his knowledge. I looked at him now, after being bucked off, and it didn't take me long to figure out he was sure enough hurt. I got my Dodge diesel pickup and loaded him into it, and for the second time in three or four hours, I had a man headed to the hospital in Flagstaff. Only this time, I would make the delivery.

To my knowledge, cell phones had not been introduced to the cowboy world, so I got on the two-way radio and told the manager I was headed to town with another injured man. While sitting at the Copper Cart Café in town gossiping, he had already told people I was hard to work for, and now he didn't sound happy, as if it was my fault. I didn't care, I was getting the cow work done, and all he was good for was answering the telephone, so I drove to the hospital.

About seven o'clock that night the doctor informed Tom that his shoulder and collarbone were broken, and he bandaged him up real well, and gave him a large prescription of pain medicine, and sent us on our way, telling us that Tom needed to stay immobile for a month or so, and his shoulder would heal in time.

Tom preferred painkiller that could be bought in a liquor store, so we purchased a supply of that along with the Percecet. While Tom was in the store acquiring these items, I communicated, via radio, with the manager and learned that Barney had been air-vaced to Barrow's Neurological Center in Phoenix and had been put on life-support in an intensive care unit. Pat and Debbie, his mother, were in route to Phoenix to be with him. The manager also informed me that he had hired two new hands, and they were spending the night in the guest house adjacent to my home in Seligman. I was supposed to take them to the wagon in the morning. Perhaps he thought they could replace Pat, Barney, and Tom.

Tom and I got to Seligman in time to catch a couple hours sleep, and then at 3:00 a.m. I got up and roused Tom and the new additions to my crew. One of these was a boy named Jessie, who claimed to be 18 years old. In fact I learned later that he was 15 and had just run away from home, which was somewhere east of Arizona. Jessie was a very nice looking boy and was very quiet and polite. He was obviously under considerable stress, trying to act both knowledgeable and brave. The other man was named Eric, and he was proud of his nineteen years on this earth and didn't mind telling you so. He stood about six feet three inches and 200 pounds, opposed to Jessie's five foot three inches and 140 pounds. Eric's hair was the color of carrots, and the bone above his eyebrows was at least an inch thick. Before the day was over, the cowboys waiting for us at Hazen Hole had nicknamed him Eric the Viking. We all loaded up in my pickup and headed north to the wagon, which by the road was some 60 miles or so distance. The doctor had ordered Tom Reeder to go home and rest, and beings his teepee was the only home he had, he was going with us.

We got there about 5:00 a.m., and I introduced the new boys to the crew, who were all up drinking coffee; Jessie disappeared into a shadowy corner of the cook tent and said nothing, while the Viking made his presence known by dragging his size 13 boots on the dirt floor, stirring up enough dust to choke everyone until they all went outside, except the cook, who was frying breakfast and therefore held captive and getting madder by the minute.

As soon as we ate breakfast, someone wrangled horses so I could catch Jessie and the Viking something to ride. The crew had caught horses the night before but did not know that two new men were coming. I had only been wagon boss since the October before, and there were still some horses I didn't know, so I asked everyone if they knew of an extra horse that was sure enough gentle to mount Jessie on. Everyone on the crew was as new as me, with the exception of Pat Prosser, who was in Phoenix, and Truman Rustin, who had worked for the outfit off and on for years, so I relied on Truman's advice.

Truman was 60 years old with wavy silver hair and sparkling blue eyes. He resembled the movie star Richard Farnsworth. He was always clean shaven and neatly dressed in spite of the primitive living conditions, and knew how to set his hat at the perfect angle in order to accentuate his virile profile. He was a lady's man, and of late had been visited by a certain good looking nurse from Prescott named Connie. He had told everyone they were married, although that proved to be untrue. My wife had met Connie, who was a very nice lady. One day the telephone rang at our home and my wife answered. A female voice on the other end said, "Hello, I would like to get a message to Truman, if that is possible."

My wife responded, "Hello, Connie, this is Jean Ann."

The phone went quiet for a long time and finally the voice asked, "Who is Connie?"

Truman believed in the old adage, "To thine own self be true." and his loyalties ended there. When I asked him about a gentle horse he pointed out an old bay gelding named Teddy. He claimed that Elmer McDonald, who was a very good hand, but recently retired, had ridden him for years. He guaranteed me he was gentle, so I caught him.

For Eric the Viking I roped a big glass-eyed paint named Patches. Patches had spent some time in a bucking string, but supposedly had quit bucking, but was a little hard to get on. The Viking assured me that he could mount anything that had hair, and when he put his bridle on him, I advised him to ease up on him and keep his spurs out of him. I turned my attention back to Jessie, who seemed to be having trouble getting the kid horse bridled and saddled. For a saddle, he had an old flower-carved antique with a Bob Crosby tree and round skirts that was probably made in the 1940s. But his bridle was brand new having a chrome-plated bit with JAPAN stamped on it. At first I couldn't figure out what was wrong and then realized that the reins were connected to the headstall end of the bit, and the headstall was connected to the reins end. The curb strap was upside down and attached to the wrong end. I ran to my truck and got some pliers and began tearing the bridle apart so I could reassemble it correctly, when I heard a thunderous fart, and I turned around in time to see the Viking being launched into the stratosphere by Patches, the ex-bucking horse. The Viking's one point landing measured 5.5 on the Richter scale.

It was getting light and I was getting mad knowing that the sun would come up and find me and my crew still in camp, a fact I did not appreciate. I noticed Floyd the cook and Charlie the Indian horse wrangler standing outside the cook tent observing the goings on. The cook was slapping his leg and laughing hysterically, while the Indian was staring with typical Indian stoicism, wondering how a bunch of white skins, who were so stupid, could have possibly killed all the buffalo. I got Jessie's bridle straightened out and helped him get saddled up, assuring him that old Teddy was gentle. "Just get on and wait for the rest of us to get mounted and we'll go gather some cows." I told him, trying to be friendly because I liked the little runaway who looked like Chris Shivers, the famous bull rider. I turned around to give Eric some riding instructions and realized I hadn't even gotten saddled. About the time I threw a blanket on my own horse's back, I heard a scream and turned to see Jessie hit the ground shoulder first and witnessed Teddy jumping and kicking through the community of teepee tents. I thought to myself, I swear I'm going to castrate that old silver-haired lady's man!

As someone ran and caught Teddy and another went and counseled the little runaway, I got saddled and witnessed the second launching of Eric the Fearless. The cook now lay in the dirt laughing, and Kawliga simply stared in amazement. I called a universal time-out and instructed Jessie and Eric to lead Teddy and Patches through the gate and not mount up until I gave them further instructions.

I led my horse through the gate and called Truman aside and, in a quiet voice, told him I was going to beat him until blood ran out of his ears if Teddy bucked with the runaway again. "When he gets on, you get a hold of his bridle reins and lead him around like he is your grandson, but whatever happens don't let him get bucked off again!" He was mad but gave me a slight nod to the affirmative. I turned to the redhead with lots of bone in his forehead and told him to keep his spurs out of Patches. "We've got lots of work to do, and I don't have time for you to learn how to ride!" I insisted. The sun was now up, and though I was in a hurry, Patches had decided he was not going to cooperate. Eric the Viking had bravado but, certainly, no horsemanship skills, and Patches wouldn't stand still long enough for the clumsy redhead to get on. I asked Randy Rutledge to hand me his catch rope, which I put around Patches' front feet and instructed him to dally up and jerk Patches on his side when he tried to step away from Eric. I explained to Eric what was going to happen, telling him to act like he was going to mount up, and when the horse tried to whirl away to just get out of the way while Randy laid him down. An application or two of that, and the outlaw would stand still.

We laid ole Patches out a couple times, and then I hobbled him with my pigging string, and I took Randy's rope off his front legs. I told Eric I was going to stand by Patches' head and hold on to the bridle reins while he mounted. I further explained that once he was mounted I would reach down and unhobble the horse. Before proceeding any further, I explained in great detail that if he would get on, and hold his reins tight with his left hand, and hold the saddle horn with his right hand, and simply stand up in his stirrups, keeping his spurs out of Patches' belly, that the old horse would gladly walk off without trying to buck. I leaned forward until our eyes were only 14 inches apart and said very clearly, "Eric, do you understand?" He assured me that he did. Right before I leaned over to untie the hobbles on Patches' front legs, I notice Jessie mounted on Teddy a few feet away. He was crying, and Truman's blue eyes were sparkling. The Viking stepped onto the old paint horse's back as I held the bridle reins. "Are you all right?" I asked the redhead. "Remember, keep your spurs out of him; just stand up in your stirrups and let him walk off!" I leaned over and took my pigging string off of Patches' legs and then the Viking threw his right hand up to the sun and lifted both legs bringing them down with toes turned out in a spurring motion that brought another large expulsion of gas from the backside of the paint horse, and within two jumps Eric was slammed face-first into the middle of a hard dirt road.

This time he began to scream as if someone was skinning him alive starting at his scrotum. He lay on the ground and rolled over and over wailing in agony, holding his stomach one second and his head the next. I had had enough of Eric and hoped he would die. To say I gave him a cussing would have been an understatement! I leaned over his writhing form and told him in great detail what I thought of his actions, and in very descriptive language told him how stupid he was. And then suddenly, as I stood over him hoping we could soon have his funeral, he jumped up as if ready to run back to the line of scrimmage. He faced me, and with a great show of exclamation, he folded his arms, and threw back his head at a haughty angle, and loudly proclaimed to everyone present, "Well, I'm just an old boy trying to make a living!!!"

I stood in utter consternation! I was speechless. I was so completely taken aback after that performance that my mind went blank for awhile, and I don't remember exactly what happened for 15 or 20 minutes. Somehow or another we all got mounted (there were about 14 of us) and started trotting west to where I wanted to start my drive. Clarity of mind came back when we were at the top of a hill, a mile or so southwest of camp. I looked back and realized that Jessie was a quarter mile behind and having a hard time keeping up. I asked, even pleaded with, Truman to take care of him and not let him get hurt. I sent half the crew with Randy, including Eric, whom I was sick of, and I took the other half going north, and we began making a drive toward Number Nine, three or four miles away. I left Truman and Jessie in the middle.

Our morning gathering went well, and we managed to gather three or four hundred cows, and as they went through a gate into Lower Sandstone Pasture we paired them out, making sure each cow had her calf with her and turning back those that were not straight. We did this as they were strung out and moving and managed to make fast work of it.

As the last cow went through the gate, I asked Truman where Jessie was. "Oh, he's all right," Truman replied. "He just doesn't know how to ride and he's moving slow." I looked out in the direction Jessie should be coming from and saw a horse and rider coming a quarter mile away. We started loping that way and soon came upon the runaway, who was riding humped over and leaning over the saddle horn. "Are you all right, Jessie?" I asked as I rode up next to him. His hat was pulled down on his forehead, and added to the fact that he was leaning forward and I could not see his eyes. He did not reply. "Jessie, are you all right?" I demanded. He didn't reply, and I leaned over trying to look into his face that he lowered even farther. I thought I detected a faint whimper. "Jessie, you need to talk to me, or I'm going to slap the crap out of you!" I shouted, and with that he slid off the right side of the horse and landed in a fetal position on the ground.

Holy smoke, I've killed the kid, I thought to myself, and jumped to the ground and hovered over him trying to figure out if he was dying or crying. I asked questions, and he wouldn't speak. I could tell he was breathing but could not tell if he was conscious. "Jessie, talk to me!" I pleaded. I sat down on the ground, and picked the boy up in my arms, and held him like a baby, "Jessie, tell me where are you hurt?" He wouldn't utter a sound with the exception of the occasional whimper. I finally resorted to threats of physical violence if he didn't start talking, which seemed to be the only thing that made him act rationally. I finally got him to say that he had a deep agonizing pain in his abdomen.

About that time Floyd Martin, the cook, and Charlie Wascogomie, the horse wrangler, showed up in my Dodge pickup. Floyd had asked me that morning if he could use my pickup to go to Rose Well and get a couple of barrels of water for the wagon, and while he was there, he and Charlie could take a shower in the bunkhouse there. They were returning to camp, and when they stopped to see what was going on, I loaded Jessie and myself. When we got to camp, I unloaded the water, cook, and horse wrangler; and Jessie and I headed west toward Flagstaff and the hospital some 100 miles distance. For the third time in less than 24 hours, a man on my crew was headed to the doctor. Wow, I thought, what a rough outfit!

Going west from Hazen Hole, you pass through the Redlands Camp on Babbitt's W Triangle Ranch and travel over, at least, 45 miles of poorly maintained dirt roads before you reach the highway. Jessie curled up and lay tightly against the passenger door refusing to communicate. Every time I would pass over a large rock or bump, he would let go of a bloodcurdling scream that would raise the hair on the back of my neck. I did not know if I should drive fast or slow, so I drove fast. The only time the boy would respond to a question was when I would ask him if he was dying, to which he offered a very faint, "Yes, I think so." I wasn't sure.

Around 1:00 p.m. I pulled up to the emergency room door of the Flagstaff hospital and ran in and announced that I had possession of a dying boy. Several minutes later I sat exhausted in the waiting room contemplating the romance of being the wagon boss on the biggest outfit in Arizona. I wondered why Bill Owen didn't paint a picture of me dressed in my cowboy regalia as I sat in a Naugahyde chair reading "Redbook" and calculating how much canyon fodder I had left to feed to the enemy as we charged forward.

Several hours later, a doctor in a white gown came out leading Jessie, who was moving. I saw no bandages, "How is he," I inquired?

The doctor pulled me aside and talked in a low voice, "He's fine."

"What? You didn't have to operate or something? No internal bleeding?"

"No, he's just pretty shook up and a little bruised, but he's going to be fine." The doctor turned around and disappeared into the bowels of the new building that was being financed by industrial compensation insurance.

We headed back to camp taking the same route back through Kendrick Park, Valle, and Redlands. I wondered how I should handle this situation, thinking my batting average had slipped several digits in the last two days.

The next morning we ate breakfast an hour before sunup, and after consuming lots of black coffee, I started out of the cook tent toward the corral where we had a fresh mount of horses waiting. I eased toward Jessie and told him I needed to talk to him in private. "Jessie, I need you to stay here and hood for the cook." I told him quietly.

"What's 'hood for the cook' mean?" he asked.

"That means, help the cook: like wash the dishes, and chop wood, and pack water, that sort of thing." I replied. I liked the kid, and if he wanted to run away from home that was none of my business, but I didn't want to get him killed.

"I quit!" Jessie answered defiantly.

"What in the world are you quitting for?" I demanded.

"I am way too good a hand to be a hood!"

The author catching horses on an Arizona cow outfit.

Clay Ashurst on Sparrow at Pica Camp, 1995.
Photo by Margie Fancher.

ഇ൭ⱳ

Wild Horses,
Wild Horse Riders
and Rides to Remember
ഇ൭ⱳ

*"You know that expression, 'wild horses couldn't drag me
away'? Well, let me tell you, that was obviously made by
someone who's never been on the other side of a lead rope
when a wild horse starts running."*
Terry Farley

One day in March of 1971, I drove up to Sand Flat on
Marion Perkin's Bar Cross Ranch, and about the time I
rolled to a stop between the camp house and barn, I saw
a sorrel horse packing a saddle and dragging some hackamore
reins running down a sandy wash towards camp. I had just gone
to work for the outfit a few days earlier and had been moved
to Pine Flat, another cow camp a dozen miles to the north, and
had driven to Sand Flat to talk to Mike McFarland, the ranch
foreman. About the time the riderless bronc reached the horse
corral, Mike rode up on a chestnut horse he called Jim Beam and
roped the sorrel and proceeded to lead him back up the canyon
to the man who owned the saddle that was on the loose horse's
back. Within a few minutes the sorrel horse came into view a
second time, and this time Gar Holbrook was on top of him. Out
in the middle of the draw, which becomes wider and flatter near

the campsite, there stood a lone juniper tree that was quite large. The tree stood about a hundred yards southwest of the barn, and Gar and the sorrel, whose name I learned later was Burrhead, were trotting along at a brisk pace pointed toward the lone tree. About the time the bronc rider and Burrhead were a step or two from the shade of the tree, Burrhead broke in two and bucked under the tree where a limb scraped the man off his back. This time, the second within 10 or 15 minutes, hitting the ground injured Gar, and Burrhead was turned out to pasture until a later date.

Several months later Mike told me the whole story of that day's events, which unfolded like this: Gar had ridden Burrhead in the cedar picket round corral for a couple of days preceding the day I just described. And then on the morning of the third ride, Gar mounted the colt that was four years old, and made several revolutions around the corral, and announced "outside." Mike, who was mounted on Jim Beam and had plans of hazing for Gar, opened the round corral gate, and turned Gar and the colt into the wide open spaces. The cowboy and colt trotted out of the corral, and turned south for a moment in front of the barn, and then headed east up the bottom of the sandy draw. As you traveled up the draw, it narrowed and its sides became steeper and after several hundred yards turned into a canyon, the walls of which were covered with a good spattering of juniper and pinion trees. Up the bottom of the canyon Gar traveled, with Mike following a few yards behind and Burrhead purred along in a trot, as happy as a horse could be. After maybe a quarter of a mile, Gar turned the colt up the left slope of the canyon, and they gained altitude continuing on at a trot. After traveling uphill at a gentle angle for several hundred yards, the horse and rider reached the top but were stopped by a continuous rimrock about four feet high. The rimrock had the effect of a fence, which held you under the canyon rim, and Gar continued on riding directly under the canyon rim with the steep canyon wall dropping to his right. After a spell, Gar and Burrhead found themselves traveling on a bench with the straight rimrock continuing on their left and a shorter rimrock on their right. And then, suddenly, the bench narrowed and came to an end. The rimrock on the left was like a straight wall, four or five feet tall, and the one to the right was straight off three or four feet, with the canyon wall sloping at a 45 degree angle below that.

Burrhead stopped there, having nowhere else to go but down, which was pretty much straight off. Gar was riding the colt in a hackamore with a rawhide bosal and heavy braided split reins made out of strands from an old nylon rope. He pulled on the left rein trying to coax the horse into a tight left hand turn so they could exit the cul-de-sac the same way they had entered. Burrhead did not respond, so Gar pulled on the right rein and managed to get the bronc's head turned a little but his feet did not respond. Actually, Mike, who was watching a few yards behind, had never seen the cowboy turn the horse completely around. For three days, including this one, he had mounted, and as long as the colt moved forward he had left him alone, not trying to turn him at all. Now, Burrhead was getting sulled-up as Gar pulled the rawhide noseband one way and then the other, trying to turn the colt around with no results. The colt's nose was getting sore, the cowboy was getting frustrated, and nothing was being said except a little profanity under the bronc rider's breath, or a wisp of confusion in the bronc's mind. And then, thinking it would coax the colt into action, Gar lifted his left leg and drug a spur out of the bronc's left shoulder.

Wow! Nothing but clear blue sky was under Burrhead now after that initial jump to the right. It was 200 yards to the bottom of the canyon with quite a few trees in between. Mike watched in pure disbelief as the horse bucked, squealed, and farted off the side of the canyon. A horse jumping as high as he can straight into a 45 degree slope can gain a lot of altitude. Mike told me at times the horse and rider would disappear on the downhill side of a tree and then would reappear sailing completely over another tree as the mad colt bucked out of control going down, down, down. With each jump Mike thought the horse would fall and the man would lose his seat. But every time they reappeared, they would be connected and flying like a bird.

When Burrhead and Gar got to the bottom of the canyon, they landed in deep sand in the creek bed, and Burrhead fell and then jumped up and ran off leaving Gar lying in the sand but uninjured. Mike, who is one of the better cowboys I've known, said he never witnessed anything that compared to the man and horse going down the canyon slope. Mike rode up to Gar, who was white as a clean sheet, and asked, "How did you ride that son of a gun?" Gar looked up and with trembling lips replied, "I had to!"

Meanwhile in Nevada...

In the spring of 1963, Little Ben Fancher and Jimmy Miller, who were 19 and 15 years old, respectfully, arrived at the Quarter Circle A Ranch at Paradise, Nevada. The Circle A, as it is known, was, and is, one of the biggest ranches in the West. The ranch was known for having its fair share of horses that were hard to ride. Ray Winters, the wagon boss, eyed the two young cowboys from Arizona with, if not skepticism, certain indifference because he had a crew and was short on gentle horses to mount an inexperienced button. "What kind of horses can you boys ride?" the wagon boss asked as he stared at the two boys.

"The saddle maker in Prescott, Arizona, that made my saddle said it fit any horse's back, and my ass fits that saddle!" was Ben's reply, which was quite a statement coming from a boy who owned no reputation. The reputation and, eventually, legend would come later; and perhaps started there. I heard that story from Ben and Jimmy, both, many years later, and on different occasions; and I also heard it from Gene Ericsson, who showed up at the Circle A several weeks later, and they all told the story the same. Ben backed up his rash statement and soon had the respect of Ray Winters, who was a legendary bronc rider himself.

Gene Ericsson told me he saw Ben take one of the Circle A's worst buckers, a horse named Wino, and after spurring the hair off of him, cinched him up real tight, and roped several fat dry cows on him. A few applications like that and the horse got gentle. Roping some big heavy cattle on an outlaw horse and letting them get jerked around for awhile has gentled more than one outlaw. The Circle A had a number of great bronc riders come and go in those years including Ray Winters, Frank Lebioux, Tommy Tyree, Gene Ericsson, Jimmy Miller, and Ben Fancher. Dave Ericsson worked all over Northern Nevada and was also well known for his bronc riding skill.

Jerry Chapin, who is one of Nevada's best cowboys, told me that the day before Christmas Eve in 1967 Dave called him on the telephone. Dave was running the Rancho Grande north of Elko for Walt Whitaker. "Come on over tomorrow, Jerry, and we'll ride some bucking horses." It was very cold as only Elko County can get, and there was lots of snow on the ground. Jerry informed Dave that he wasn't interested in riding bucking horses in the snow on Christmas Eve. "No! No!" Dave replied, "I got a couple of kids here, and they're going to ride 'em, and we'll just watch." Jerry was working for Jimmy Wright over the mountain near Tuscarora, but he agreed to drive over and watch Bob Scott and Jeff Prosser, who were about 18 years old, ride the broncs. The corrals at the Rancho Grande were on a slight slope, and the livestock that were in them had packed the snow into a solid sheet of ice. By the end of the day, the crew had bucked out every available horse on solid ice and uneven ground with no one getting hurt.

I worked in Elko County in 1973 and was repeatedly asked if I knew Dave Ericsson and Ben Fancher. People were still talking about their riding skills.

Charlie Chapin's brother, Harold, gathered lots of mustangs over the years and loved doing it. Charlie told me about a time Harold went out mustanging by himself, because all of his mustanging buddies were busy doing something else. He went north of Winemucca, near a spot called Blue Mountain, and roped a big mare with his rope tied hard-and-fast to the saddle horn. Harold got the mare jerked down and was sidelining her with some shackles (a short piece of rope with horn knots braided in both ends). He got one end of the shackle around a front ankle and was trying to get the other end over a hind foot when the mare got the bulge on him and got up. In his struggle to keep the mare held down, and a horn knot applied front and back, the loose end of the shackle pulled up tight around the palm of Harold's hand. One of Harold's hands was connected by a foot or so of rope to the front foot of a full grown mustang. The mare was trying to kick Harold every way but loose, and he was thinking that perhaps he had met his demise, when a little slack was thrown into the lasso and Harold's saddle horse set back real hard. When the mare hit the end of the rope, the mare's neck was broken saving Harold's life. Charlie told me that Harold laughed when telling the story, but didn't go mustanging by himself anymore.

I was working for Charlie Chapin at the Gilmore ranch 70 miles north of Wells, Nevada, in the O'Neill Basin. Charlie and his wife Lois were two of the finest people I've ever known. Lois would cook sourdough pancakes for Charlie and me every morning and they were always perfect. I was breaking colts to ride, and Charlie gave me a big five-year-old bay horse named Gem Bar. Gem Bar had been bucking someone off around there, and they had turned him in, and the horse needed to be broke. Gem Bar bucked a couple of times, but really just needed someone to camp on him and give him a job.

One Friday Charlie suggested we load up in the trailer and go north to Idaho to a team roping. So the next morning, being a Saturday, we loaded our horses and drove north to Rogerson, Idaho, and there turned west and drove to a place called Three Creeks. There was nothing at Three Creeks but a one room schoolhouse and a ranch headquarters with a nice roping arena. A large crowd made up of mostly ranch people had assembled, and the team roping had about 130 teams entered. Charlie won the team roping heeling for someone that I didn't know. They also had a calf roping, which I entered mounted on Gem Bar. There were a total of eight calf ropers, and when it was my turn I nodded, and Gem Bar and I came out of the box; but after about twenty feet the big bay blew up and went to bucking. I was riding him in a snaffle bit and spurred him harder with each jump because I could hear the folks on the sideline screaming and clapping. Gem Bar finally decided to run after the calf, and I tied him down in 37 seconds and won first, which paid a whopping

$3.50. Charlie and I went back to Nevada feeling like heroes with enough money to buy supper at the casino in Jackpot as we drove home late at night.

Over at Palo Duro Canyon...

Mike Landis, whom I have worked for three times, told me that he was working at the J A's in Palo Duro Canyon when Boots O'Neal came to work there in 1949. Mike claimed that every man that worked there had a horse or two that would buck; some had more than one or two. Mike said the crew knew Boots was coming and the string of horses he was going to get

Pieface and Boots at the Tin House - *by Mike Capron*

had more than its share of sure enough broncs, so everyone was anticipating what fun it was going to be watching the kid get farted off. It didn't happen because Boots, though only 16, could ride them.

I worked with Boots when he was in his fifties and he was still capable of riding a bucking horse. I had started a colt at Babbitts, where Boots and I worked together, I called Pieface.

Pieface was not an outlaw, but he would buck when he was fresh. He stood about 15 hands and weighed 1,150 or a little more when he was mature. Pieface never bucked me off but he was hard to ride, at least for me. He had a way of rolling in his hide when he jumped that felt funny, and it would make your saddle roll around and feel loose.

Bill Howell, the wagon boss, put Pieface in Boot's string, and I saw the horse buck with him two times, and he seemed to ride him easy both times. The second time we were working yearling heifers in the shipping pens at Tin House on the W Triangle Ranch. Boots was on Pieface and he roped a 600 pound heifer with his rope tied hard and fast to the horn, and Pieface blew up and went to bucking and spinning. The corral was not much wider than the length of Boot's tied lasso, and Pieface wasn't just goating, he was sure enough bucking hard. The old Texan put on a superb show, riding the bucker while, at the same time, continuously throwing the slack of his tied lasso up in the air, sometimes behind him, to keep the out of control horse from getting rim fired and tangled in the rope. When Pieface quit bucking the heifer was still out at the end of the rope, and Boots and the horse were not fouled up by the rope in any way. It remains one of the best displays of real cowboy skill I have ever witnessed.

Boots told me he broke 200 colts to ride before the age of 16. He rode a bronc to school and then rode him home when school was out. His horse breaking helped supplement the family's income. He told me one winter he and another cowboy stayed together in a camp on the Matador Ranch in Texas and broke about 60 broncs. They caught and saddled a new bunch every Monday morning. They started five apiece, riding them Monday through Friday, and took the weekends off, and then started a fresh bunch the next week. After five rides the colts were considered broke and ready to put into the remuda. Boots did this several times on different Texas outfits.

Anyone with much experience with horses will agree that a colt that has been ridden five times and then ignored for several months might be harder to get along with when he gets caught again to be saddled and ridden. Many ranch colts might get a good start but then not be finished well. People now days watch countless hours of horse shows on TV hosted by superstar trainers like Pat Parelli, Clinton Anderson, and other guys. They make a good living demonstrating how to teach a horse to push a large beach ball around an arena with a roof on it. In the real cowboy world, on a big ranch, a man with a saddle didn't have the luxury of a covered arena, and plenty of time to lunge his colt, and entice him with sugar cubes and whispers. The boss caught you a horse and led him out to you, and perhaps it was raining, or snowing; if it was morning, it was probably pitch black, and you were expected to be saddled and ready to ride in minutes. The crew wasn't going to wait around while you lunged, or prayed, or tried to get yourself in the mood. You got saddled and got your behind in the saddle, or you didn't keep your job. If the horse happened to be a four-year-old that had been ridden a total of five times several months earlier, that was your problem. You were wearing a cowboy hat when you asked for a job and that meant you claimed to have the ability to cope, and those who couldn't cope didn't last. I'm not saying that the old ways, in which Boots and men like myself had to abide, were always conducive to good horsemanship, and I'm not belittling those who train horses to push beach balls with their noses; I'm just telling it like it was, and still is, in some places. When you worked for Whistle Mills, Mike Landis, John Andrews, Bill Howell, Bob Burris, and Charlie Chapin, and others like them, you saddled up and got on and rode; and if your horse wasn't cooperating you coped the best way you could, but you better keep up and keep a leg on each side. How you did it didn't matter as much as just getting it done.

Out on the Cataract Plains...

In late winter and early spring of 1971, the Diamond A Ranch north of Seligman had a big horse roundup on the north end of the ranch on what is known among cowboys as the Cataract Plains. The Diamond A, or Boquillas as it is sometimes called, is bordered on the north by the Supai Indian Reservation, and the Hulapai Indian Reservation on the east. Hundreds of horses owned by the Indians had been running wild on the Boquillas for years until finally Jim Lowrance, the ranch manager, got the brand inspector, the tribal council, and Indian police to agree to gather and sell all of them. The Indians weren't using them anyway. The Diamond A crew eventually gathered over 500 wild Indian horses and corralled them so the tribe could sell them.

One day, while running horses in a big roundup, Dave Ericsson, who was part of the Diamond A crew, roped a seven-year-old bay stud, and, with the help of several other Diamond A cowboys, rolled his saddle under him and rode him to the wagon that was camped several miles away. Dave named the horse Prisoner, and I never saw a horse that was more aptly named. Dave castrated him and broke him to ride.

In the fall of 1973, I worked on the lower wagon on the Diamond A for Mike Landis, who was the wagon boss. I asked Mike to put Prisoner in my string. He stood about fourteen and a half hands and might have weighed 950 pounds soaking wet, but he was what cowboys call a big little horse, meaning he had lots of heart. I heard he had bucked quite a bit when Dave first started him, but he never bucked with me. He wasn't gentle, but if you watched your manners, he would watch his. I loved him: he was quick footed, and easy traveling, and tougher than a 16 penny nail. He didn't want petted or curried. When we were camped on the south end of the ranch he would act like any other horse in the remuda, but if we were camped to the north near the plains where he was raised, he would separate himself and walk the horse pasture fence staring off to the north.

We camped at a place known as Shafer and gathered 1500 steers and put them west into a pasture called Trinity. After that was done, Mike moved the wagon to Keseha 10 miles away, and as the cook, hood, and horse wrangler moved the camp, the cowboy crew made a big drive in Trinity, gathering the steers we had put in there from Shafer plus many more. We started on the northeast corner of Trinity and gathered the west half of the pasture down through Cooke Dam and Horseshoe. There were eight of us in the crew, and we gathered 20 or 25 sections of rough country with lots of trees and put 2500 steers through a gate into Black Mountain Pasture. In defense of Mike Landis, the wagon boss, he was doing it this way because he had been ordered to by the manager. It was brutal; I ran the wagon there 20 years later and would take four or five days to gather the same country with more men. One Texan cowboy came riding up to me and another fellow, cussing us because we wouldn't flank over and help him a mile or two away. I laughed at him because we were all badly outnumbered and tired. I was riding Prisoner.

It was about five miles from where we finally turned the cattle loose to Keseha where we were going to be camped. Mike Landis was famous for traveling at a fast trot everywhere he went, but he walked the five miles to camp. I couldn't have made Prisoner go any faster if I had tried. Bob Scott was riding a tough yellow horse called Scotch, and when we reached camp Bob unsaddled Scotch and turned him loose. Scotch took a big drink of water and walked out from the corral a hundred yards and fell over dead. Prisoner ignored the water trough, and slowly walked a couple hundred yards, and stood hip shot with his head down for a couple hours, looking like the proverbial "End of the Trail" painting. Finally, toward the evening, he walked back to the trough and watered out. Three days later he was as good as new, his instincts telling him how to survive.

Over in New Mexico...

In the spring of 1974, I worked for Bob Burris at the Gray Ranch in Hidalgo County, New Mexico. It was the first spring Bob managed the Gray and it was extremely dry. I remember for a spell the ranch was feeding 10 semi loads of protein blocks a week to supplement the cow herd. We shipped lots of cows that spring to other ranches the company owned.

Jim Dolan, whom I had known from Northern Arizona, was also working there. Johnny Davenport was the jigger boss. An old man named Buck Moorehead lived at the Adobe Camp with his wife. Buck might have been the best cowboy on the ranch, but he had asked Bob if he could cook for the wagon, and he did an excellent job. Bob ran a good outfit in my opinion, and in spite of some extraordinary problems facing the operation due to the severe drought the area was suffering, things went smoothly.

There were about a dozen men with the wagon. The horse wrangler was an old wetback from Chihuahua, who was a good fella, and there were two other Mexican cowboys: Gabriel, a tall athletic blue-eyed man who was very competent, and a man named Ray Martinez. Ray was supposed to be the bronc man for the outfit. He was surly and unfriendly and had, as my friend Pat Lauderdale would say, shifty eyes. I did not trust him.

Ray Martinez was more afraid of a horse than most men I have worked with, especially for a man who claimed to be a colt rider, or bronc man. He had a small Appaloosa horse in his string that was about five years old that he was absolutely terrified of. When he would get ready to mount him, his hands would be trembling, and it would take a considerable amount of dancing around, trying to get ready, for him to finally mount up. The Appaloosa had him figured out seven different ways. He would ride the Appy in a homemade braided horsehair hackamore that was one piece, plaited together. It was quite a piece of work but very ineffective. One day we had a big herd of cattle thrown together, maybe 300 cows, in the bottom of the valley, south of the Gray headquarters several miles. It was hot and windy, with dust blowing in our faces creating a lot of mud in our eyes and dirt in our ears. It was miserable. Ray, the bronc man, was riding the ole Appy and was on the backside of the herd where all the gunsels like to be, because there is less action there, and you're not required to think. He was wearing a very large coat, and by the time we got our roundup thrown together it had warmed up, and all the rest of us had rolled our jackets up and tied them behind the cantle on our saddles. Ray hated to get off of the Appaloosa because he was hard to get on, and he was so terrified of him, but he wanted to take his heavy coat off. He finally mustered the courage to take the coat off while staying mounted, which required working very gingerly as if he was defusing a time bomb. Keeping the coat very close to his body so as not to spook the Appaloosa, who was continuously snorting and looking around, Ray got the coat in front of him and rolled it up. He then put it behind the cantle and tied the right side of it with the saddle strings. Next he had to temporarily turn loose of the coat and twist his torso to the left so he could secure the left end of the coat with saddle strings on the left side of his saddle. In that second when neither hand touched the big coat, a great gust of wind, coming from his left side, picked the untied end of the coat up and over the horse's hip and it dangled all the way to the ground at the bronc's right hind foot. YeeeeeHaw!!! The race was on as ole Appy left the gate so fast that Ray's face turned Oriental due to the great force of wind pulling his eyes into a slanted expression. Bob Burris was in the middle of the herd trying to cut out a cow as the Mexican and dragging coat split the roundup in two pieces resembling a microscopic film of an egg or a cell splitting in two. Jim Dolan hollered, "Maybe so poco tiempo queire vamanos." and the bronc man and the Appaloosa disappeared over a ridge, horsehair hackamore and all. He came back about an hour later wearing the coat.

There was another horse in Ray the bronc man's string called Diablo. Every big ranch I was ever on had a certain horse that was only talked about in hushed tones and whispers. The attitude of a crew can resemble a saloon full of hard drinking men when the worst hombre in seven counties walks in with the demeanor of a man looking for a fight. All of a sudden everyone is looking at the floor and trying to act like "El Hombre" didn't really walk through the swinging doors. Sometimes it's the opposite with the crew hooraying and kidding the man who needs to mount "the bad one." Nobody said anything to Ray about Diablo, but after the wagon had been working for three weeks, Ray had still never called for and ridden the horse. Diablo was a good looking blaze-faced sorrel with a flaxen mane and tail that stood 15 hands and weighed about 1,150 or 1,200 pounds. He was 10 years old and Ray had been riding him for five years. Legend had it that Diablo would buck the man off any time he took a notion: one time, supposedly, the bronc man hit the ground 10 times in one morning, but because of his great sense of duty he kept him in his string.

The wagon was camped at San Luis Pass, which is on the Continental Divide four or five miles north of the Mexican border. One evening before Buck Moorehead the cook hollered chuck, a Border Patrol pickup pulled up to the wagon and arrested Juan, the old horse wrangler, Gabriel, and Ray the bronc man. Juan and Gabriel were back within 36 hours, but Ray decided to vacation for about 10 days. When Ray returned Bob put him to work with the "mud gang," or ranch construction crew. To my knowledge Ray never worked as a cowboy at the Gray again.

Bob asked me if I wanted to ride Diablo, and I said I would. An old cowboy named Buzzard, who had been working for "the Company" his whole life, told Bob the outlaw horse would kill me if I tried to ride him. In Buzzard's opinion the man didn't live that could punch cows and make a hand on Diablo. The wagon moved to a camp called the Culberson Place where the fateful showdown was to take place. Oren Rainey and his wife Quincey lived at the Culberson. It was still pretty dark when we saddled up, and everyone else was mounted when I stepped on the famous outlaw. I lifted my right leg and stuck a spur as deep as I could between the cinches on the right side, and the battle was on. Diablo bucked pretty high in the front for two or three jumps, and then took his head and bucked off in a straight line. When he was done bucking, I was still on and he had some visible spur tracks on him including some deep ones on his shoulders. Later on, Bob took me aside and told me I could spur him anywhere I wanted, as long as it was behind the front cinch. "Company" policies forbid spurring a horse in the shoulder. Buzzard was mad because I had bested his pet outlaw. Actually, on a scale from one to ten, with ten being a real great bucker and one being a dink, old Diablo was about a five. I rode the horse through the rest of the roundup, and he only bucked two more times and only half heartedly at that. Diablo wasn't anything to brag about and riding him wasn't either.

On the morning I and the man I was traveling with left the Gray, a gal named Agnes cooked breakfast for the two of us in the bunkhouse. She and her husband had worked for the Company for years. She confided in us saying that she and some other old-timers on the outfit were going to call the owner of the outfit and get Bob fired because he didn't know what he was doing. A few months later she and her crew of mutineers were gone and Bob was still there. Good for Bob.

And in Arizona...

When I was young and getting started as a cowboy, the ranch in Arizona that had a reputation for bucking horses was the Babbitt outfit north of Flagstaff. The widely circulated story about Frank Banks, who was the Babbitt Ranch manager at the time, bragging about killing three Indians at Flagstaff's All Indian Rodeo and Powwow, is actually true. Logue Morris, a well-known Arizona cowboy in his day, was paid to be arena director at that big Fourth of July blowout for years. Logue and Frank were good friends, and for several years Logue talked Frank into supplying the bucking horses for the Powwow. Frank would haul several truck loads of Babbitt brood mares into the rodeo. For the most part, they were older mares that were about to be culled, and none of them were broke to ride, likely not even halter broke. The year that was so hard on the Indians was probably 1964. Ed Banks, Frank's son, remembers Bill Howell hauling the mares to the fairgrounds and visiting Frank and Logue at Logue's camp after getting the mares unloaded. Bill went to work for Frank in October of 1963, and Ed Banks remembers Bill being new to the outfit when the event took place.

In the first couple rodeo performances, two different Indians met their fates getting bucked off Babbitt mares. Large doses of liquor probably contributed to their demise. Toward the middle of the rodeo, which stretched out over several days, bronc riders quit showing up to compete. Toward the end of the rodeo, possibly the last performance, a well-known Sioux bronc rider came out of the chute in the bareback riding. The man knew he had the event won if he made a qualifying ride of any kind, due to the fact so many cowboys had "turned out," which is rodeo lingo for not performing. The mare bucked straight toward the grandstand with the Sioux bronc rider in total control. When she reached the fence in front of the grandstand, she turned, bucking down the fence toward the catch pen end of the arena. When she reached the end of the arena, she tried to jump the fence into a small corral with the rider still attached. She successfully completed her discipline (pun intentional) with the exception of hanging her front feet between the two boards on the far side of the jump. This fact had the same effect as fore-footing her with a lasso, which brought the mare crashing down on her back and breaking her neck, as well as the neck of the Sioux bronc man who died with his hand still in the bareback rigging. Number three.

The dead bronc rider's body was removed posthaste by paramedics on the scene, but the mare remained untouched while the rodeo went on as usual with a large crowd seated in the grandstand. Several hours after the performance was over, Frank Banks and Logue Morris were visiting at Logue Morris's camp a quarter mile away from the arena. Two Navajo squaws approached the camp and asked Logue if they could have permission to butcher the dead mare that still lay where she and the Sioux Indian had fallen. Logue gave Frank a questioning glance, and Frank said sure, that was fine with him. Nothing was wasted.

In 1967 I went with my family to watch the powwow and rodeo at Flagstaff. As part of the rodeo they had a wagon race. The rodeo arena was in the infield of an oval racehorse track of standard size about a mile in length. There were perhaps five or six wagons in the race, each with a two-horse-hitch pulling a buckboard with rubber truck tires instead of wooden-spoked, steel-rimmed wheels. Several wagons had one man on board, while others might have five or six Indians in the wagon. There seemed to be no rules.

My dad and I were standing directly behind the rail in between the second turn and the finish line, which was about 150 yards to our right. In the exact instant the pack went by us, a buck Indian fell off the front seat of a wagon and landed behind the right hand horse. This happened less than 40 feet from where we were standing. The wagon was going as fast as two horses could pull it, and both tires on the right side ran over the man's head. The wagon bounced sufficiently to make the two squaws, who were in the bed of the wagon and obviously intoxicated, laugh slapping their legs with glee as they were jostled about. To the astonishment of hundreds who witnessed this happen, the inebriated man stood up and walked off even though his entire head was as red as a tomato.

One time in the mid '70s, I was at an Indian rodeo at Tuba City on the Navajo Reservation. Bill and Harvey Howell and I went up there and entered the team roping. We were sitting on our rope horses near a gate between the roping chutes and a large covered grandstand that was packed with spectators, all of them Indian. A bareback rider got bucked off the left side of a bronc and was severely hung up. The pick-up men were not mounted well, or perhaps were inexperienced, but for whatever reason they didn't catch the bronc or help the rider. The man got kicked every way but loose, besides getting scraped against fence posts, as the pick-up men chased the bronc making him wilder as the event drew on. Finally the man and horse separated right in front of the grandstand. He lay limp and still for a good while, perhaps a minute, and no one walked out to help him. The people in the grandstands, probably three or four hundred, became deathly quiet, you could have heard a pin drop. Causally two Indians went out to assist the bronc rider, picking him up, putting his arms around their necks, and helping him toward the gate. The bronc rider was a very handsome man, who weighed about 140 pounds, and was wearing a beautiful white cowboy shirt with pearl snaps that now had blood stains in several places. He was conscious when the two men helped him up. The crowd in the grandstand remained silent and attentive. Then suddenly, after the bronc man took a half dozen steps, his body went limp as he passed out, and the grandstands erupted into the loudest and most hilarious laughter I ever witnessed.

Back on the ranch...

The most fantastic buck off I ever witnessed happened at Cedar Ranch, a Babbitt cow camp 35 miles north of Flagstaff. I had only been working for the outfit a week or two, and it was around the first of June, 1974. One of the cowboys in the crew was a man called Gordon who hailed from Malta, Montana. Gordon was riding a big five-year-old sorrel named Paiute, who weighed about 1200 pounds. Every one mounted their horses in the quakey aspen corral, and then Bill Howell opened the gate and took off at a long trot. Cedar Ranch sits at the foot of a high malpai rim that rises about 500 feet, gaining altitude right out the backdoor of the bunkhouse. The opposite direction, which is north, the country continues to slope downward for another quarter mile emptying out onto open and rolling limestone mesas that stretch as far as the eye can see. The trail Bill was leading us on was a very rocky slope. I was the last one out the gate and Gordon was right in front of me. As soon as Gordon and Piute got outside the gate, the big horse blew up jumping and kicking straight over his head. The first jump was straight, but with the second one he turned a quarter uphill and kicked over his head again. The third jump, Piute turned to the left again, which now had him facing downhill, and his front feet were a couple of feet off the ground; but in the act of turning, his hind feet were not only kicking high but turning to the right or opposite of his front end, which created a vortex of stupendous proportions. Gordon had been bucked off from the get-go, but wasn't completely disconnected until this third jump. All of this was happening on a rocky hillside that sloped up on the left, and as the horse reached the maximum height of this third jump Gordon, involuntarily, kicked over the cantle and became airborne. The runway was a long way away, and it was strewn with jagged black malpai rocks about the size of cantaloupes. He landed on his knees and the palms of his hands, and when he stood up he held out his hands, palms up, and all of the hide was gone.

The best...

Bob Scott was the first really great bronc rider I cowboyed with, but I have known many since then. Ken and Coy James could ride as good as anyone of my generation, and I saw them prove it many times. Milo Dewitt can ride in the brush as well as the arena, and placed in the bronc riding at a pro rodeo way after his 50th birthday. He was Turquoise Circuit champion several

Matt Shiew at the Arizona Cowpucher's Reunion Rodeo. Photo by Kathy McCraine.

times. Clay Tyree won the bronc riding at the cowboy reunion in 1980 on the famous gray outlaw from the Double O Ranch that had come close to killing Joe Chavez at the Soto Camp only several months earlier. One of the best cowboy bronc rides I remember was Gary Halford on a paint horse at the reunion in the mid eighties.

All of my life I've heard old men talk about how the horses were ranker in the good old days. I think the opposite is the

This Page
Above: Olin Borg. Photo by Kathy McCraine.
Right: Dally Burt. Photo by Sally Bates.

Following Page
Top: Clancy Goswick. Photo by Kathy Mc-Craine. Bottom right: Cody Lesueur. Bottom left: Bronc rider. Both photos by Sally Bates. All Photos on both pages at the Arizona Cowpuncher's Reunion Rodeo.

truth. When you watch old films from rodeos of yesteryear, the consistency of great horses doesn't compare with those of today, or so it seems to me. There have been some truly rank buckers in every generation, but there are lots of them today. There are some young bronc riders today that are as good as any that ever lived. Among the ones I know personally are Garrison, Cooper, and Miles Dewitt; Tyler Rice; Tell Good; Everett Ashurst; and

Facing Page: Everett Ashurst at the Arizona Cowpuncher's Reunion Rodeo. Photo by Sally Bates.

Above: Miles DeWitt at the Arizona Cowpuncher's Reunion Rodeo. Photo by Sally Bates.

Matt and Ben Shiew. The toughest bronc riding to win, in my opinion, is at the Cowpuncher's Reunion in Arizona because the horses supplied by Milo Dewitt (who has a great bucking horse breeding program) and Scott McDaniel are ranker, and they make you ride with one free hand, and you're disqualified for losing a stirrup. These rules, whether anyone likes it or not, causes the cream to rise to the top.

In September of 2012, Milo Dewitt asked Everett and me to come to Roswell, New Mexico, and pick-up broncs at a rodeo where he was furnishing the broncs. The folks at Roswell had put up a sizeable amount of prize money, and they bucked 50 broncs in one Saturday night performance. It was a first class event, and Milo had brought the A team, and the crowd wasn't disappointed. Two horses jumped out of the arena, and one boy from Texas got bucked off so hard it knocked him out cold.

Some boys were riding with a night latch, which is a

Facing Page: A bronc rider at the Arizona Cowpuncher's Reunion Rodeo. Photo by Kathy McCraine.

Above: Everett Ashurst making a good ride at the Arizona Cowpuncher's Reunion Rodeo. Photo by Sally Bates.

handhold tied to the fork of the saddle. Any good night latch man I ever saw tied it very tight to the saddle, making it difficult to get their hand between the handhold and the swells. Several boys at Roswell had night latches tied real loose, which had the effect of being out at the end of a long whip. Their arms were stretched out, and every one of them lost control of their heads, and it started flopping around and pretty soon their feet went over their heads, and they ended up in a somersault an Olympic gymnast would be jealous of. A real loose night latch on a Milo Dewitt bucking horse is much worse than no night latch at all.

Matt Shiew, from Ashfork, Arizona, was the only man to get both of his broncs ridden at this event, and he did it the

Facing Page: A bronc rider flying high at the Arizona Cowpuncher's Reunion Rodeo. Photo by Kathy McCraine.

Above: A cowboy makes a good ride at the Arizona Cowpuncher's Reunion Rodeo. Photo by Sally Bates.

Matt Shiew at the Arizona Cowpuncher's Reunion Rodeo, Williams, Arizona. Photo by Kathy McCraine.

correct way, with his free hand off to one side and his other hand handling his rein like a real pro. Matt Shiew can ride a bucking horse in a stock saddle as good as anyone who ever lived.

Meanwhile back on the ranch...

In the summer of 1976, I started some colts at Cedar Ranch in between the spring and fall roundups at Babbitts. One of the colts was a big streak-faced sorrel I named Ranger. Ranger was out of a stud that belonged to Frank Banks who, although retired as Babbitt Ranch manager, still ran some mares on the ranch. For the most part he just gave his colts to the company. The stud Ranger was out of was notorious for throwing colts that had a little buck in them.

The first day I messed with Ranger I got on him and he didn't want to untrack, but I got him to buck a little, and in doing so I got a little forward motion out of him, a jump or two at a time. The second day, regardless what trick I tried on him, I could not get him to move. He would simply stand still with his head in the air staring off into space. I turned loose horses into the corral with him, and me on top whipping, spurring, pleading, and screaming to high heaven; and he would not move a muscle. I was by myself and I finally gave up. The third day I got Harvey Howell to help me. Harvey had a big stout horse he called Marlboro who was incredibly stout pulling something by the saddle horn. I put the stoutest halter I could find under my snaffle bit headstall, and Harvey got on Marlboro and took the lead rope and dallied up. Marlboro could pull a bogged down train out of a swamp, and he began dragging Ranger with me on top, and we headed out the infamous gate where Gordon had gotten bucked off Paiute. We got out the gate about 60 feet, and Ranger was still locked up tighter that a drum with figure eleven drag marks behind us about two hundred feet long, and then the lead rope broke. Ranger had been setting back, and when the lead rope broke he stood straighter and was as still as a bronze statue. Harvey spurred Marlboro into a lope, and went around behind me, and then turned and ran by me, and squalled like a wild Comanche hoping Ranger would come unlocked and follow him.

Whew! That did it! Ranger had a spiritual awakening and came unlocked, unglued, and plugged-in all at once. The trail from where the lead rope broke went another 100 feet and then fell off a tank dam at a 50 degree angle about 20 feet to the bottom. After that you picked your way through several hundred yards of very large thick boulders going through two gates, that thankfully were open, and found yourself in the horse pasture that was about a square mile in size. In about 30 seconds Ranger and I were in the middle of the horse pasture, and the amount of bucking and stampeding it took to get there, I don't know, but I know it didn't take long. It was exhilarating!

And in Cochise County...

Fred Davis is a cowboy and horseman of note whose family has ranched in Cochise County for several generations. He told me this story that happened before he was of note. Fred was about 17 years old, and was starting a colt that was particularly skittish, and was not long on brain power. He had ridden him two days in a row in the bronc pen, and beings it was the third day he had plans to go outside on him for the first time. His father, Houston, had instructed him to check on a particular first calf heifer that was in a pasture adjacent to camp, so he had a mission, which is always a good thing when riding a colt.

Not too many days before this took place, Fred had acquired a pup that was about grown, and he had plans on making a cow dog out of him. He had heard many tales about old-timers who were good dog men necking a pup to an older dog, who would then teach by example. Fred necked the new pup to an older dog, both of which were wearing heavy collars. He used a stout piece of parachute cord to accomplish this, leaving the dogs three to four feet apart.

Fred mounted the bronc, and after making several laps around the corral, he opened the gate and let himself outside with the freshly connected dogs following. He and the colt took off at a fast pace looking for the first calf heifer, and everything was going fine. After making it a quarter mile or so out into the pasture, he heard the dogs erupt into a convulsion of barks and yelps, and after much effort, got the colt to slow down enough to look back and see what the ruckus was about. The two dogs had gotten themselves tangled up in a Mormon tea bush. Fred called to them and gesticulated instructions but, if anything, the nylon cord got more wrapped around the bush.

He started backtracking and stopped his horse about 10 feet away from where the two dogs stood wagging their tails and hanging their tongues out, something dogs are very good at. Fred wondered if he was going to have to dismount to fix the problem

Fred Davis of Cochise County: Collaboration of Training Techniques
- *by Mike Capron*

---

when suddenly the dogs made a particular maneuver and things began to change. Fred saw a vision of things to come, but was incapable of changing the course of history. His muscles became inert, like he was in a dream with some monster attacking him; but he couldn't make his body move.

The dogs got themselves untangled from the Mormon tea plant, but in their exuberance they immediately tangled themselves up again, wrapped around the bronc's hind leg. Things were a fast blur for a good while but, miraculously, everyone survived.

Back at the Diamond A wagon...

Many a good cowboy has filled in as cook on some outfit when the steady cook becomes unavailable due to sickness or some emergency. More often than that, there is no cook at all, and a crew may take turns filling the vacancy until a steady man can be obtained to do the job. There was a particular cowboy working at the Babbitt Ranch one time who agreed to do the cooking for the roundup until a real cook could be found. This individual ended up cooking for close to a month, until, much to his relief, he was finally able to get back horseback.

Several years later this same fellow became manager of the Diamond A Ranch to the west of Babbitts. The Diamond A is Arizona's biggest ranch, although Babbitts is a not too distant second. The management position on the "Big Boquillas," as the Diamond A is sometimes called, suited this hombre fine, and he allowed that he had been given the position due to the fact he was king of the cowboys.

There was at the time a cowboy working at the Boquillas named Dale Lee, who was a character of noted qualities, the least of which was the fact he was wild as wild can be. Dale had red hair and a big handlebar moustache and he always wore a big black hat. He resembled the cartoon character Yosemite Sam. Dale had cowboyed all over four or five states and had devoted his life to being the fastest, wildest, buckenhorse-ridenest, specimen of a cow-chaser that ever lived. He had been successful. He wasn't, necessarily, what you would call smooth, but he was wild; and he didn't care who liked it or didn't.

There was a young boy working with the Diamond A wagon who became especially enamored with Dale, thinking surely he was the greatest cowboy who ever lived. He listened in reverence to everything Dale said. One evening the crew was sitting around the B. S. fire outside the cook tent waiting for Rex, the cook, to holler chuck. The manager, who could be described as a big shot, was there.

"Dale, what about that Babbitt outfit; you worked there didn't you?" The boy asked Dale.

"Yeah, I sure did, and it's a good outfit too."

"Well how big is Babbitts, Dale? Is it a big outfit?" The boy queried.

Left to Right Alvin Wagner, Perry Blankenship, Leland Larson, Slim Gillium. Diamond A Ranch circa 1960. Photo courtesy Marvin Davis.

"Big outfit!" Dale exclaimed loudly. "Let me tell you somethin' boy! The man that runs this outfit used to be the cook over there!"

The manager suddenly needed to get in his pickup and go home.

The wagon moved to the 7s...

For many years the Diamond A ran two wagons. I was working for Mike Landis on the lower wagon, and we were camped at the 7s Ranch 20 miles north of Ashfork. Alvin Wagner and his wife Hazel were living at the 7s at the time. Alvin was the 7s camp man many years, and was one of my favorite people, and one of those men who never lost the sparkle in his eyes. He was devoted to Hazel and she to him. They never had any children. Alvin was a good cowboy, and better than average roper, and like all men of his generation who had hailed from east of Arizona, he was a hard-and-fast man.

We had just moved to the 7s and got our camp set up when we received word that the cow buyer, who had bought the outfit's yearlings, was going to show up early in the morning and help us gather steers the next day. He sent instructions that he wanted to borrow one of Alvin's horses to ride. We were catching horses in the evening and feeding them hay in a corral at night, and Alvin told Mike Landis to rope ole Chinate for the big shot to ride when he got there in the morning.

It was early November, but we were up drinking coffee in the cook tent at 4:00 a.m. when we heard the big shot's pickup drive up. He entered the tent with a hail and a hoorah, and soon every living thing within a mile knew he had arrived. He loudly inquired to Alvin about what horse he was loaning him, and Alvin explained that they had caught him Chinate. Alvin, who was not beyond pulling a prank, had actually been generous because the black horse was as good as any on the outfit. The big shot immediately exclaimed that it was a good thing because he figured there would surely be an opportunity to rope a wild steer before the day was out, and he was no doubt the best roper within several counties. Alvin smiled and took a puff on his Bull Durham cigarette, saying that perhaps there were others present who could rope just as well. More hoorahing and loud talk, mixed with considerable bragging, and soon everyone was in a gleeful humor waiting in anticipation for the day's events to unfold.

We were saddled, and slapping leather long before the sun came up, and headed south in a long trot with Mike Landis and the big shot in front and the rest of us two abreast and following; several miles south of camp we crossed under the Santa Fe railroad and kept trotting to the back side of a pasture called Eight Mile. We split up in the order the wagon boss wanted with instructions to meet at a dirt tank that had the same name as the pasture. We had gathered about 500 steers, and the plan was to cross them under the railroad and trail them to a holding pasture near camp.

The big shot had been a swell fork, full double man all of his life, but because of the influence of a hand he admired, who had been to the northwest, he had recently been converted to slick fork saddles, long ropes, spade bits, and lots of silver. At that day in time, Ray Holes of Graingeville, Idaho, was considered to be one of the premier saddle makers in the west. The big shot had a new flower-carved Ray Holes saddle that was actually silver and gold mounted. It was built on a 3B tree with about a nine inch fork. It had silver conchos and a silver cantle plate with a gold steer head. The tall dally horn had a silver horn cap with fancy gold filigree overlay: to say it was beautiful was an understatement. It was reported to have cost $3,000 while at the same time you could get a new John Herron or Scott Deiringer saddle for $300.

We trailed our 500 Mexican steers to the bridge going under the railroad, and had been instructed by the wagon boss to make a hand because the steers were not going to want to go under the railroad. More than one wreck had happened trying to negotiate this maneuver. Bob Scott, who was the jigger boss, was on the right point and I was on the left, and it seemed like there was electricity in the air as we approached the bridge. The steers were ringy and plenty nervous, but everyone was at the top of their game, and as soon as the leaders slipped into the shadows of the bridge the rest followed as if they had been greased. As the last few were about to pass under the bridge the big shot conveniently let one turn back. It was the moment he had talked about all morning, and with a loud squall, John Wayne would have been proud of, he pitched ole Chinate the slack and took up in hot pursuit. The Mexican steer had high horns and weighed about 700 pounds. When he saw he had been given the chance, he put a figure nine in his tail and took off like a buck deer. Chinate laid his ears back and took to him like he had been eating corn, and very soon the horse had the Mexican within easy shooting range. The newly converted slick fork man cut loose with a big blocker and roped the Mexican deep. Quite possibly, every critter that had ever been caught on the black horse had been caught on a tied rope, and like any good horse used to a tied rope, as soon as the lasso went over the steer's head he locked up; butt down, shoulder and neck up, the horse slid to a stop expecting the jerk that didn't come. The big shot was packing a long rope expecting to dally, but instead, when Chinate shut 'er down the man went crotch first over the silver and gold horn cap severely scraping his testicles and other hanging apparatuses in the same vicinity. He came to a stop with arms around the horse's throat latch and knees in front of the saddle. Someone had to go retrieve his rope along with the Mexican.

That was the day I learned that silver horn caps with large mountings of sharp-edged gold filigree are a bit impractical.

And then back to Pica...

"I'm tellin' ya, Larry, life just ain't fair!"

"What? What in the world are you talkin' about, Cole?"

Cole and Larry were rooming together in a teepee on the Diamond A wagon, close to forty years ago, and they had turned in early. Lighting a lantern, Larry was laying on his back reading a Louis La'mour shoot 'em up. He thought Cole had fallen asleep. Cole's sudden outburst startled him.

"Well, it's like this," Cole continued in his slow Texas drawl, "I been layin' here thinkin', worried sick about that bronc I gotta get on in the morning! I probably won't get an ounce of sleep tonight knowin' I cain't ride 'em if he bucks in the morning! And that bronc, he's out there in that corral, eatin' hay, just plumb happy. I'm the last thing that's on his mind. And I been laying here listenin' and I can hear that bronc Tim Prosser's gonna get on in the morning! He's pacin' back and forth, walkin' up and down that fence! He won't eat, and he's worried sick thinkin' about what might happen to him if he so much as looks sideways when ole Tim gets on 'em! And that durn Tim Prosser, he's laying over there in that teepee sound asleep. Just as peaceful as all get out! I'm telling ya, Larry, life just ain't fair."

Buck Moorehead, Gray Ranch wagon cook. Photo by Kurt Markus.

Sam Fancher riding one right, brogan shoes and all. Photo courtesy Patti Parker.

Uncle Ben

The trouble is not that I am single and likely to stay single,
but that I am lonely and likely to stay lonely.
Charlotte Bontë

Forty years ago the man who was generally considered to be the best cowboy in Northern Arizona, at least by the people that I knew at the time, was Ben Fancher. Actually, the name Ben Fancher could be confusing because there were two Ben Fanchers roaming around the country at the same time. The man I just spoke of was "young Ben" or "little Ben," and the other cowboy with the same name was "Uncle Ben" and was young Ben's uncle. Young Ben's parents were Eph (pronounced Ē f), who was Uncle Ben's older brother, and Ada Fancher. Uncle Ben was born in 1917 on the Big Sandy River in Mojave County; young Ben, or little Ben, was born in 1943. Little Ben was actually much bigger than Uncle Ben standing about five feet eleven and weighing 180 or 190, whereas Uncle Ben stood about five foot seven and weighed around 145 with his chaps and a heavy coat on. They were both cowboys and bronc riders extraordinaire.

Uncle Ben was the youngest in a litter of pups who all made their mark in one way or the other in the cowboy world. Eph cowboyed around Arizona, California and Nevada; and like a lot of his contemporaries, he didn't tend to stay anywhere very long. He could generally go back and find a job on any outfit he had left because he was a hard worker and consummate cowboy and horseman. Another brother, Sam, migrated to California and Nevada, and was equally well known for his cowboy skills, and

They Were All Kid's Horses to Uncle Ben - *by Mike Capron*

was the father of Sammy Fancher who became a world champion barrel racer. A sister in the family named Myrtle married Dallas Yarbrough, and her son Jim was a much respected cowboy in northwest Arizona. Everyone in the family was noted for being expert horsemen, and ropers, and very skilled at gathering wild cattle.

Uncle Ben was a character in the first degree. He was noted for possessing a carefree spirit. Sometimes his joking could get him in trouble. On the Fourth of July, 1941, Uncle Ben was entered in the bronc riding at the Prescott Frontier Days rodeo. Andy Juaregui was the stock contractor, and he always halter broke his bucking horses. Andy would tie all of his broncs to a long picket line and feed them hay while they were tied up. Uncle Ben and a friend were walking around behind the arena one night after the rodeo performance was over. They had a bottle of whiskey in their possession and were looking for some excitement. Ben untied Andy's best saddle bronc and led him over to the edge of a carnival that was set up adjacent to the rodeo arena. With the help of his friend, he jumped on the bronc bareback and drug a spur out of his neck with the horse pointed toward the Ferris wheel. After several wild strides, Uncle Ben lost his mane hold and rolled off the bronc's hind end, and the horse kicked him as he was falling off. Everyone thought Ben was dead.

Ben's sister Myrtle, who was in Kingman at the time, got a phone call and was told, if she wanted to see Ben alive, she better get to Prescott fast. Myrtle got her son Jim to drive her to Prescott at breakneck speed, hoping to speak to her brother before he passed on. When Myrtle and Jim got to the Prescott Hospital, Ben was nowhere to be found. He had been lying unconscious on a gurney in a hallway of the hospital when he woke up. Nobody had informed him he was dying, so he simply got up and walked off unnoticed. Myrtle found him down on Whiskey Row.

In 1941 Ben came close to winning the world in saddle bronc riding and probably would have if he would have tended to business. More than once he won first at a rodeo and several hours later gave his trophy buckle to a little kid he ran onto on the street. He liked to ride but cared nothing for notoriety or record books.

Uncle Ben was drafted into the army in January of 1942 and became part of the U.S. Army's famous 32nd Infantry Division, which by the end of World War II had seen more combat than any outfit in United States military history. Ben was involved in heavy fighting until the end of the war and was a participant of the "Long Road Back" from Australia through New Guinea and on to the Philippines. He fought at Buna when the 32nd became the first American division to launch an offensive against the Japanese in New Guinea. It was at Buna that the division won a Presidential citation, and the right to wear the Distinguished Unit Badge. Ben fought at Saidor and Aitape and was a veteran of the bitter fighting in the Ormoc Corridor on Leyte. He saw action on the Villa Verde Trail, high in the precipitous Caraballo Mountains in northern Luzon.

On one campaign Ben was forward on reconnaissance with orders to find the enemy. He and another soldier began seeing lots of enemy tracks, and sent word back to their commanding officer that the enemy was near, and perhaps setting up an ambush. The officer argued, not believing the recon men's advice because they had not encountered the enemy in a number of days. Ben was an expert tracker because of his years cowboying and continued to warn his superiors that the enemy was near. The officers would ask in unbelief, "How do you know for sure?" To which Ben would reply, "Because there's sign everywhere. I know they are here!" The officer refused to listen and marched his men into an ambush, and Ben barely escaped with his life. Ben fought continually for over three years, and like many others he suffered immensely.

In a way Ben treated rodeo and the Army the same. He entered the Army as a private first class, and at the end of the war, he was still a private first class; and yet, his accomplishments as a soldier were significant enough to have an article written about him in the *Arizona Republic* newspaper. He could ride broncs as good or better than anyone, and he could fight and soldier like a hero, but he said little. Trophy buckles and stripes on the sleeve of a uniform meant little to him.

Ben wrote lots of poetry and wrote this poem while stationed in New Guinea.

Uncle Ben on Paiute, Tucson Rodeo, 1941. Photo courtesy of Sam Yarbrough.

Uncle Ben on Whiz Bang, Klamath Falls, Ore., 1941. Photo courtesy of Sam Yarbrough.

Somewhere in New Guinea
By PVT. Benjamin Fancher

Somewhere in New Guinea where the sun is like a curse,
And each long day is followed by another slightly worse;
Where the brick red dust blows thicker than the shifting desert sand,
And the white man dreams and wishes for a fair and greener land.
Somewhere in New Guinea where a woman is never seen,
Where the sky is never cloudy and the grass is never green;
Where the dingo's night howl robs a man of his blessed sleep;
Where there isn't any whiskey and the beer is never cheap.
Somewhere in New Guinea where the nights are made for love,
And the moon is like a searchlight and the Southern Cross above
Sparkles like a diamond necklace in the balmy tropic night,
It's a shameful waste of beauty for there's not a girl in sight.
Somewhere in New Guinea where the mail is always late
And a Christmas card in April is considered up-to-date;
Where we never have a payday and we never have a cent,
But we never miss the money 'cause we'd never get it spent.
Somewhere in New Guinea where the snakes and lizards play,
Where a hundred fresh mosquitoes replace each one you slay.
So take me back to Arizona; New Guinea fare-thee-well,
For this God-forsaken outpost is a substitute for HELL.
Amen

Arizona Republic article, including poem, courtesy of Sam Yarbrough

When the war ended, Ben took up cowboying and riding broncs where he had left off. Perhaps whiskey was now a more constant companion, but he kept the war and his emotions to himself and continued to look at life on the light side.

There was a girl south of Kingman whose father owned a big ranch where Ben had worked from time to time. She had her eye set on Ben and chased him vigorously for years. He liked her as a friend, but refused to go down lover's lane with her in spite of her good looks or attention. One day he called her on the phone and told her he had built her a house in Kingman and was ready to set up housekeeping with her. She jumped in her car and met him at an arranged spot, and then together they drove to a lot that Ben owned on the edge of town. Ben had set up his canvas teepee tent, which measured eight foot by eight foot, and told her he was ready to pick her up and carry her over the threshold. She got the message, Ben wasn't the marrying kind.

Ben roamed around cowboying, making lots of trips to the big outfits in California and Nevada. One time he found himself broke and out of a job in the San Joaquin Valley where he managed to procure a job on a large farm. The farmer put Ben on a tractor pulling a seed drill. The farmer showed Ben how to fill the seed hopper and gave him detailed instructions on how to operate the machinery and then drove off leaving Ben driving up and back in a very large field. After an hour or so the farmer returned to check on Ben's progress, and after stopping him he walked behind the tractor and checked how much seed was left in the hopper. It was empty, and the farmer launched into a tirade, jumping up and down on his hat and cursing profusely at the incompetence of the man on the tractor who wore a big black hat. Totally unconcerned Ben drawled his reply to the man's emotional outburst, "Hell, I wasn't planning on being here when it came up anyway."

Ben was working for some people in the Hualipais helping them gather during roundup. The country was steep and rocky and choked with every variety of brush and thorn known to grow in the state of Arizona. The cattle were fast, and in that country only an expert can expect to hold them up or corral them. One day a bunch of cattle got the jump on Ben who gave hot pursuit for a long time, and had he had a good hand backing him up, he would have stopped them, but eventually they cleaned his plow and got away. He pulled up, and unsaddled his hot and sweaty horse, and sat down to smoke a Bull Durham cigarette.

The rancher for whom Ben was working was also the man who had failed to flank for him, which allowed the cattle to escape. "Ben, I think you're slippin'!" the man commented when he finally caught up and found Ben dismounted and smoking his cigarette.

"Yeah! I can slip a long way and I'll still be ahead of you. You */-#*/!"

Ben would wear a big hat with the brim rolled up on both sides in a classic cowboy crease. Underneath the hat his small and wiry frame, even in old age, had the consistency of rawhide, and he stepped like a man capable of quick work. He drank

Uncle Ben at the O RO Ranch in 1974.

too much but I never heard of him being vulgar. He would tip his hat when meeting a lady and would control his tongue. He had the habit of biting off more than he could chew when he was drunk, and would end up on the bottom of the pile in the frequent scrapes in which he found himself. During one fight an opponent broke his nose and moved it permanently to one side of his face, where it rest on a cheekbone. And yet he bore his deformity with grace, and in one of those odd mysteries of nature, the broken nose was almost a positive addition to his uniqueness. He was like a twisted knot in beautiful hardwood

Jessi Can Make It - *Mike Capron*

---

that when cut, varnished, and fashioned into part of an expensive piece of furniture ceases to be a knot but, instead, a piece of art. I never saw him when he wasn't clean shaven, and his bronze complexion and athletic countenance under the big cowboy hat made one think the mold had been broken when he was made. There was only one Uncle Ben.

In 1970 Uncle Ben worked for Bill Howell on the Babbitt Ranch in Northern Arizona. One of the horses in Ben's string was an outlaw named Jessi James. Jessi had been a notorious bucker and difficult to get along with. Ben liked him and the horse seemed to like Ben, and didn't give him the trouble he had given most everyone else. Ben wasn't afraid of him, nor did he baby him or walk easy around him. Ben wasn't a horse whisperer in the phony modern sense of the phrase, but he understood and respected horses and he didn't fight them. He just made a hand and otherwise left them alone. The wagon was camped at Redlands, and one morning the crew loped six or seven miles north of camp in the Little Redlands pasture. Ben had been quiet all morning and everyone had pretty much forgotten he was even there. He was riding Jessi James. Bill and all the crew rode up to the edge of Cataract Canyon and looked off into it.

This is a beautiful part of the Grand Canyon drainage that few people ever see and is about 20 miles south of the Supai Village and Havasu Falls. The cowboys paused for a moment to admire the beauty of the canyon and surrounding countryside. Ben had ridden Jessi up to the very edge where a 1500 foot cliff dropped directly under Jessi's nose. "Jessi, can make 'er!" was the first thing he said all morning.

Little Ben Fancher circa 1975. Photo courtesy of Jim Fancher.

Charlie Chapin on Tucker winning the Hackamore Class at the Elko County Fair, 1958. Photo courtesy Chuck Chapin.

Charlie Chapin Was
A Cowboy

Show me your horse, and I will show you what you are.
Old English Saying

Each of us experience watershed moments in our lives.
We never know when we meet someone what kind of
impact the person might have on our future. I met Bob
Scott and Twister Heller in April of 1972. Twister injured his
knee several months later and had to quit working for a spell
while recuperating from the knee surgery, which resulted from
the injury. Bob Scott and I worked together for quite a while
and I learned a lot from Bob. Bob could rope a wild cow in a
bad place as good as anybody. One time a bunch of yearlings
scattered on us at a place called West Split on the O RO. Bob was
riding a black colt named Berrie and he liked to buck a little. He
wasn't particularly hard to ride but he would take his head and
buck. Bob was about to rope a 600 pound yearling and Berrie
decided to blow up and buck. Bob just reached out and roped the
yearling on a tied rope whether Berrie liked it or not, and the jerk
the yearling gave him made ole Berrie pick up his head and pay
attention. A lot of gunsels sit on barstools and talk about doing
stuff like that, but only cowboys actually accomplish the task.

Bob was from Elko, Nevada, and had done a lot of
cowboying up there and would tell me stories of places like the

25s, and TS, and Circle A. I had to go see it. So, in June of 1973, I ventured north driving a 1967 Ford Galaxy that was a running machine. There was no speed limit in Nevada in those days, and you would be going down the highway doing 80 miles per hour, and a car would pass you and be out of sight in two minutes. I left my folk's place in Payson, Arizona, at 6:30 a.m. on June 6th and was in Elko before sundown.

Bob was in Elko breaking horses for anyone who would haul him one and was staying busy. He and a good Texan cowboy named Cole Moorehouse were staying at Paul Bear's ranch east of town several miles and were using the facilities there to ply their trade. Paul owned the famous Capriola Saddle Shop as well as the ranch where Bob and Cole were camped.

When I arrived in town Bob informed me that he already had a job lined up for me on a ranch northeast of town 70 or

Bob Scott Makin' a Rope Horse - *by Mike Capron.*

80 miles. He said a man named Charlie Chapin needed to hire someone to ride colts. Bob had told Charlie that I was coming up there and was going to need a job.

Bob gave me Charlie's phone number, and so within an hour or two I got on a payphone and gave Charlie a call. He told me that he needed a man who was willing to ride a half dozen four-year-olds that were started but very green. I told him I could handle the job. And then he inquired further, "Are you willing to ride them in a snaffle bit?" he asked.

"Sure, I don't care. I'll ride them in whatever you want."

And then he went on, "Will you rope on them?"

Wow! Sounds like my kind of guy, I was thinking. "Sure, roping is one thing I can handle!"

And then he said, "Good, because I can drive into Elko and hire truckloads of gunsels who can't rope on a colt." Those were his words, not mine. We made an agreement and I drove up to the Gilmore Ranch the next day.

Charlie was born on April 23, 1923, in Elko County. His father, Ed Chapin, had migrated to Northern Nevada when he was a young man and was described by Charlie as a man who could mount an old wore-out draft horse and within minutes have him tucking his nose, rolling a cricket, and be slobbering and prancing. Charlie's brother Jerry told me he had vivid memories of his father using a reata and riding a center fire saddle. Jerry said he saw smoke come off the saddle horn many times when Ed Chapin had a large critter, such as a fat cow or horse, caught and had taken his dally hueltas. Ed was a modest dresser who liked a felt hat with a narrow brim and a conservative crease. He never wore traditional cowboy boots but preferred ankle high, lace up shoes.

Ed Chapin married a beautiful girl named Alice McKnight, who came from a well-respected ranch family from the area. Together they raised five boys: Charlie, George, Vernon, Harold, and Jerry; good men and cowboys all.

When Charlie was a teenager he went to work for the Moffitt outfit. Bill Moffitt owned cattle in several western states and for a good many years controlled a large potion of Elko County.

Charlie Chapin on Dixie winning the Snaffle Bit Class at the Elko County Fair, 1955. Note the absence of flat hats. Photo courtesy Chuck Chapin.

Charlie established himself as a colt rider and expert horseman early in life and trained lots of Moffitt horses.

While staying in a Moffitt cow camp near Gold Creek east of present day Wild Horse Reservoir, Charlie began courting Lois Reed, whose father owned a cow outfit. A great deal of what was Bob Reed's Ranch now lies underwater at the bottom of the manmade lake.

When Charlie and Lois married they moved to Jiggs, and Charlie went to work for Cord Cattle Company where his father, Ed, was manager. The Cords owned several ranches and owned upwards of 3000 cows near Golconda and Jiggs, and Ed Chapin ran their operation for many years. After working for Ed on the Cord Ranch for a year or two, Charlie and Lois moved to the Rancho Grande north of Elko, which was owned by Bill Moffitt.

Charlie's uncle, Dogie Vaughan, managed all of Bill Moffitt's ranches for many years and was quite a hand on a horse himself. Occasionally, old Bill Moffitt would get on a horse and liked a good cowboy and horse as well as anyone. One day Charlie was mounted on a three-year-old snaffle bit colt while he and Bill Moffitt's crew were sorting a big bunch of cattle in a large set of corrals. The three-year-old he was mounted on was right at the stage where he was beginning to work and look at a cow. Bill Moffitt was standing there watching and complimented Charlie on the colt. There was another older cowboy there who was mounted on a good bridle horse but for some reason was easing around on him and the horse wasn't working very well. Bill Moffitt questioned the older fellow, asking him about the horse and if he was any good. He answered that, yes, the horse was a good one; and then Mr. Moffitt asked if he could get on him and ride him for awhile. Bill Moffitt had the habit of carrying an old style buggy whip around all the time, and he mounted the man's bridle horse, and administered a good thrashing to him with the whip, and sorted a few cows on him. The horse worked noticeably better under Bill Moffitt's hands, one of which held the whip. After a spell Mr. Moffitt dismounted and as he handed the horse back to its former rider he commented on the man's technique with a horse, which produced little good fruit.

After a while at the Rancho Grande, Charlie and Lois moved to the Haystack Ranch where Charlie worked for a man named Perry Holly.

After running the Haystack for six or seven years, Charlie and Lois worked on the Quarter Circle S in the Tuscarora area and then went to work for the Marvel family on the 25 Ranch near Battle Mountain. The years Charlie and Lois spent working on the 25 for the Marvels were some of their favorites, with Charlie cowboying, and for a spell Lois cooked for the crew at the 25 headquarters, which was about 15 miles west of Battle Mountain on the Humboldt River. For a time Charlie's brother Harold and his wife Rita were working there also, and Rita and Lois were sharing the cooking chores. The ranch had a large farm crew that would work separately from the cowboy crew and the Chapin girls would feed 25 to 30 men on this farm crew on a regular basis. One day the entire cowboy crew was there also, and Lois and Rita, with the help of an Indian girl, had 50 men sit down and eat at the same time. The old cookhouse where this took place was moved by the historical society in Battle Mountain and is now part of their museum there in town.

For years Charlie had been showing a few horses that he had trained for different outfits at the Elko County Fair and other places in the northwest. He also roped calves and team roped at a few rodeos in the area, all of which were held during the summer. Harold Chapin rode broncs successfully for years.

The Marvels were horsemen and lovers of good horses and horsemanship, and besides the Chapins they had, at different times, other well-known horseman around the outfit, including the Dorrance brothers.

The Elko County Fair, held on Labor Day weekend every

Charlie Chapin on Cloud winning the Two Rein Class at the Elko County Fair, 1961. Photo courtesy Chuck Chapin.

year, has for decades had one of the premier horse shows in America. In the years when Charlie was a young man, the horses shown there and the people riding them were real cowboy horsemen off the big ranches in the area. All the horses entered in the various events had to be Nevada bred horses with Nevada residents showing them. The quality of the horses shown at the fair in those years was a cut above most horse shows of that era, and to win an event there was a true accomplishment. I've been to the fair and seen firsthand the horses sliding, spinning, and working a cow. In 1956 Charlie won the Snaffle Bit Class riding a three-year-old gelding named Dixie. In 1958 he won the Hackamore Class on a four-year-old gelding named Tucker, and in 1961 he won the Two Rein Class on a paint horse he called Cloud. All of these horses were broke and trained by him while working at the 25 Ranch for the Marvel family. Charlie sold Cloud to some people in California who rode him for years in the winner's circle in the California Reined Cow Horse Circuit. Charlie sold the paint horse for twelve hundred dollars and thought that it was a fortune. Charlie also showed horses at other shows in the area and was successful.

Sometime in the late '60s, Charlie and Lois moved to the Gilmore Ranch in the O'Neill Basin, 50 miles or so northwest of Wells, where he took the cow boss job for the outfit. I showed up at the Gilmore on June 7, 1973, and started riding colts.

June 12th was a Sunday, and the evening before Charlie told me that we ought to go to the neighbors the next day and watch a big horse branding that was going to take place. "Who knows," he said. "We might even get to rope." Sunday morning was cold and cloudy, and as we drove north to the neighbors, it started snowing. When we pulled into the outfit it was evident that we were late and the festivities had already commenced. There was a crowd gathered, but where they all came from, I don't know because we were quite a ways from nowhere. There was an old roping arena with several small corrals connected to it, including an old pole round corral about 50 feet in diameter. One side of the round pen was the side of a building that had corrugated tin siding, and there were pieces of jagged and sharp metal sticking out in the corral. The arena, which was quite large, and all the adjacent corrals were full of horses: mares, colts, squealing studs, and fillies of all sizes and shapes. They would run one horse at a time in the round corral, and two mounted men, one named Quentin Kelly, and the other Varl Agee, would head and heel the horses. If they had a stud roped, he would be castrated and branded, and the mares branded. There were several teenage boys present who would wait, being perched on the top rail of the pole corral, and as soon as a horse was roped and pulled down they would bail off, and get on their heads, and help hold them while someone else did the cutting and branding. Varl and Quentin did an excellent job roping and dallying on a slick horn. There was barbeque being prepared, and while all this took place a considerable amount of moonshine was consumed, a great deal of it by the teenagers who were mugging the horses. It was one of the wilder events I've witnessed, but no one was hurt and none of the horses were crippled or injured in any way. Much to our disappointment they did not offer Charlie and me to rope. But we had a ringside seat to a first class rodeo, and ate some good food. Fun was had by all.

One day Charlie was asked to bring his crew and help brand some calves on the outfit to the east, which was owned by some people named Boise. We made a big drive that began at the top of a high bald mountain where some mustangs ran. A few mares and a stud ran down off the mountain and passed within a quarter mile from where I was riding, but I did not pursue them remembering I had been told to gather cows and not horses. We threw the small herd of cattle we gathered together and held them in a rodeer outside without the help of any fences. There were two beautiful girls in the Boise family; I thought they were about my age, and each with reddish blonde hair. I believe the sisters names were Ila and Nina and they dragged the calves to the fire by the heels dallying on mule hide. Their cows in the roundup were wearing several different brands, and the girls had to get the calves mothered-up correctly and call out the correct brands to be applied to the calves. The irons were heated in the coals of a sagebrush fire. The Boise girls did an excellent job of roping and knew their cow herd, and on top of that were mighty easy to look at.

Charlie was a smooth hand, and the days passed by without any wrecks or overheated confrontations. His knowledge of horses and horsemanship was endless, but he only gave advice if asked. If you watched him you could learn a lot. He packed about 35 foot of rope and dallied on a small Guadalajara horn and mule hide. He had a brand new Capriola saddle made on a Chuck Sheppard tree with a full double rigging. He would laugh and call it his first swell fork saddle. He told me that in all of his life he had never owned anything but saddles with the Capriola stamp on them.

He wasn't a man who habitually talked negative, but did, on several occasions, mention that he didn't like the trend taking place in Nevada that promoted fancy dress as a prerequisite to being a qualified hand. Looking at Charlie, he didn't appear any different than cowboys in Arizona or New Mexico. He wore chinks and used a spade bit on his older horses, and a hackamore or a snaffle on the young ones, but he would have been a top hand in Texas or British Columbia. He mocked the notion that a flat hat turned you into a top buckaroo. Actually, "buckaroo" was not a term I heard him use very much. He told me the reason the quality of horses and horsemanship was, in his opinion, declining on the big ranches was the fact that cowboys, or buckaroos, never stayed anywhere very long. When he was younger, men would work for an outfit several years, or even decades and keep a horse in their string from the time it was a colt until it was well finished. In his opinion a horse that had been ridden by half a dozen men or more before it was six years old didn't have much of a chance of being any good. One of the main ingredients in a good horse is consistency.

Twister Heller worked for Charlie at the Gilmore Ranch several years before I did and is good friends with Charlie's brothers, especially Harold. One of the better known cowboys and cow bosses in the buckaroo country was Twister's father, Lopey Heller. Lopey went to work on the famous ZX Ranch in Oregon when he was just a young boy. His first job at the ZX

Mr. and Mrs .Lopey Heller Paradise Valley, Nevada circa 1965.

was horse wrangler, but within two years he was made cow boss; a position he held for 13 years. The ZX was running 18 thousand cows, in those days, in the 1940s and early '50s. After working at the ZX, Lopey also had cow boss jobs on the Piute Meadows Ranch northeast of Winnemucca, and then at the Corporation Ranch near Likely, California, and the Quinn River Crossing Ranch. After his cow boss job at the Quinn River, Lopey went to work at the Circle A at Paradise Valley, Nevada, where his friend Ray Winters was the cow boss. Ray Winters had worked for Lopey at the ZX Ranch years before. Several months after Lopey went to work for the Circle A, Ray decided to quit and Lopey was made cow boss. Very few men have ever been in charge of more big herds or big crews of men, regardless if they called themselves cowboys or buckaroos, than Lopey Heller. I met Lopey when he was about 66 or 67 years old and had the opportunity to visit with him awhile. He was unassuming in both manner and dress. On his feet he wore a pair of gum-soled Redwing work boots and going upwards a pair of Levis with no belt, a long-sleeved Khaki shirt, and a black hat with the brim rolled up on both sides. There was no silver or silk to be seen on him anywhere. If you would have seen him in Guthrie, Texas, or Seligman, Arizona, he would not have been out of place.

Sixty years ago you could get an idea where a man was from looking at his saddle, chaps, etc., but somehow in the last 30 years the notion that a man's regalia is what matters has become epidemic. I've heard many Texans make fun of anybody who wears their spur straps buckled to the inside, claiming true cowboys always wear the buckles toward the outside. J. Frank Dobie's book *Cow People,* which in my opinion is one of the most authentic narratives about the old West, has a picture of Ab Blocker, who was arguably the greatest trail boss who ever trailed a herd from the Texas brush country to Montana. In the photograph you can plainly see Ab's spur leathers with buckles on the inside.

When my two boys were about nine and ten years old, a blowhard Texan came to Babbitts where we were working. I don't remember his name, but I remember he was loud, and he had high-topped boots that he wore outside his pants and the tops were yellow. He was constantly talking about roping something with his "tiger chain" tied to the horn. He kept pestering my two sons, telling them to tie their ropes to their horns and rope a bull or a big cow with their "tiger chain." He told them they would never be real men until they survived a few wrecks connected to something big with their "tiger chain." One day I got sick of him, stepped off my horse, cinched up, and then tied my rope solid. I cut a big fat cow out of the herd and told him, "Let's rope for a while." He simply stared at me and got quiet. "Come on and get your tiger chain and let's rope some!" I told him. I had every intention of jerking his horse over backwards on top of him. He wouldn't ante up. I told my two boys, who could have easily out-roped him, to stay away from him. Bill Howell couldn't stand him and called him "ole yeller top." He didn't last long.

I know from firsthand experience that when you have a lot of work to do you don't care what a man looks like or where he's from. If it's ten o'clock in the morning and you've got a thousand cows thrown together and you need to cut out 350 head and then move the cut five miles one way and the remainder of the herd several miles another direction, and then after that you need to catch horses so you can do the same thing the day after, and you hope you're not late for supper making the cook mad. You don't care what the crew is wearing. What you want, even crave, is some good experienced help, and if they are wearing flat hats, or taco shell creases, it doesn't matter. You hope there is someone out there who will help you get the job done—period.

Charlie Chapin continued to work horseback way up past his eightieth birthday. He was at the Gilmore Ranch for many years and then worked for Wayne Hage on his ranch near Tonapah. He ended his career around Battle Mountain working for his son Chuck on the Horseshoe Ranch and his brother Jerry at the Muleshoe.

Jerry Chapin told me that one day near the end of Charlie's life, the two of them were helping some neighbors at a big branding where there were a lot of people gathered around helping. There

Charlie Chapin heeling calves at a branding when he was an old man. photo courtesy of Jerry Chapin.

was one young buckaroo present who was wearing particularly outrageous regalia. He had on high-heeled boots and lots of silver, with a yard of dirty bed sheet tied around his neck. To top things off, he had a particularly large flat-brimmed sombrero with gaudy appointments all around. Charlie stopped his horse next to the man with the fancy dress and asked him, "How come you dress like that?"

And the young buckaroo replied, "I believe in preserving the old ways!"

Charlie paused and looked around at all the people present and then continued, "I believe I am the oldest fellow here and I've never seen anybody look like you!"

When I worked for Charlie at the Gilmore, the outfit had been buying colts from Charlie's brother Harold. All of the colts I rode there were horses Harold raised, and they were good ones. The year before I was there, a yearling had disappeared and everyone thought he was dead, although his carcass was never found. One day while I was working there, Charlie got a phone call from a neighbor down on Marys River to the south toward Elko. The man told Charlie that a colt had been spotted running by himself up on top of Stormy Mountain east of the headwaters of Marys River. The next day Charlie and I loaded a couple of horses in a gooseneck and drove to the southwest, to the fellow's ranch; I don't recall his name. The man owned a Piper Cub airplane, and he and Charlie loaded up and flew up into the hills trying to spot the colt, which they found on the very top of the mountain.

Charlie and I unloaded at a corral, and after opening the corral gate, we mounted and set off for the mountaintop four or

Charlie Makin' It Look Easy - *by Mike Capron.*

five miles away. When we topped out the colt was still standing there all by his lonesome and was grazing on the tall grass he was standing in. The mountaintop was open grassland at the top with considerable brush and trees as the mountain sloped downward.

Charlie had said nothing about how we were going to subdue the young colt. A colt that has run by himself for a few months can act a little crazy if not handled right, and I was thinking he might be a little difficult to rope if we got him stirred up, which I figured would be easy to do. We rode up to within 400 yards of the colt and then Charlie stopped and suggested we dismount. We turned our saddle horses broadside to the colt and stood on the opposite side and remained silent. The colt threw his head up high and stood dead still staring at us for several minutes; we stood still and watched. Finally the colt turned toward us and then took several steps and whinnied, but our horses ignored him. And then he took a few more steps and spoke again, with nothing but silence from our end. And then he struck a prancing trot, and cut the distance in half, and stopped again with his head high and ears pointed forward. We remained still saying nothing, and finally the colt loped up and stood a mere thirty feet away. Without talking we stepped on, and turned downhill, and ignored the colt; and within two minutes he was walking along between our horses, and we resumed our favorite pastime of telling stories about the good old days and other lies. When we got to the corral we rode through the open gate with the colt following, even though we never touched him or got our horses out of a walk.

Robert Redford and the other folks in Hollywood call it horse whispering, but normal folks call it making a hand. Anyway you crease your hat, you have to say that Charlie Chapin was a cowboy.

Bill Howell, CO Bar Ranch. Photo by Kurt Markus.

Bill Howell

Never speak of genius baffled, for genius is master of man.
Genius does what it must, talent does what it can.
Author unknown

B ill Howell was born November 5, 1934, the first of 10 children born to Jim and Virginia Howell. Jim and Virginia were 18 and 17 years old, respectfully. They were living near Stapleton, Nebraska, at the time, where Jim's paternal grandfather, William, owned a ranch; and Jim worked for him there. Jim's father, Merle, also lived in the area and to some degree partnered with William on some cow deals; but any partnership they were in was short-lived due to Merle's irresponsible ways, which included a drinking problem. Jim, at an early age, developed a deep respect for his grandfather, which was equaled by a lack of respect for Merle. Merle was tall, handsome, and a good hand with a horse and possessed considerable cowboy skills; but he was also an undependable carouser who lacked any true knowledge of the cow business. In Jim's opinion he was a good-for-nothing, ne'er-do-well.

When Jim first left home at the age of 16, he worked for the Abbott family, who had put together one of the biggest ranches in the Sandhills country. Jim had excellent cowboy and horsemanship skills, was a good bronc rider, and no doubt found good use of his skills while working for the Abbotts. After a short stint working for his grandfather, William, in the Stapleton area, Jim returned to work for Abbotts for a short spell and then moved on to work for Jules Sandoz. The Sandoz family were prominent ranchers in western Nebraska and would continue to be a positive influence in Jim's life for 50 years. By the time Bill was five years old, Jim and Virginia moved again; this time to a small ranch a few miles from Seneca. They were buying a small place of their own and also working for Virginia's father, Nat.

Virginia was the elder daughter of Nat and Ratia Warren and was raised on their ranch south of Seneca, and Mullen, Nebraska, in the Dismal River country, which was, and still is, some of the best cow country in America. Nat was a tall slender man, who was nervous and always on the move. If he wasn't doing something, he was thinking of doing something. The

Nat Warren's yearlings, circa 1940.

Warrens believed in putting their hands to the plow and keeping them there. They worked hard and applied themselves. They were successful.

Nat, through hard work, and with a keen business mind, had begun putting together a ranch that could eventually sustain several hundred cows. Nat was what ranch people called a good cowman. People liked him and the Warrens were well respected in the community. Jim Howell loved and respected Nat, and he wanted to acquire Nat's ability to be a successful rancher and businessman. In contrast, and on the opposite end of the spectrum of his love for Nat, was his hatred for his mother-in-law Ratia. Jim considered her to be as caustic as Nat was refreshing, and there was no love lost between mother-in-law and son-in-law.

Jim was a noted horseman and supplemented his income by trading and training horses, including training for neighbors who were willing pay for his skills as a horseman. Work horses were still used in that area to put up hay and pull feed wagons, and Jim was a good teamster and trainer of work horse teams.

Jim had a team he called Dick and Shorty that was phenomenal. In the summer during haying season, he would hitch the two horses to a beaver slide, and they would work all day long with nothing but voice commands, walking forward and then straight backward, working in unison, running the forks that raised the hay up the slide. In the winter Dick and Shorty would be hitched to a wagon that would be filled with cottonseed cake. Jim would saddle a horse and tie him to the end of the wagon and leave camp driving the wagon out into the Sandhills to feed. Upon reaching the first feed trough, which would usually be by a windmill, Jim would stop, and get out of the wagon, and fill the troughs with cake. When he got this accomplished, he would mount the saddle horse that had been tied to the wagon and gather the cattle in the surrounding area, and bring them to the feed ground. When Jim rode off on the saddle horse, Dick and Shorty would pull the wagon, unassisted, to the next feed ground, which might be a mile away. Jim would also gather cows into the second feed ground, and the team would have the wagon stopped and waiting in the exact spot where it needed to be. They would repeat this process day after day. When Bill was old, I asked him how come the team was so good at what they did, and he replied, "Because they knew the old man would beat the hell out of them if they didn't do it right."

Bill grew up riding and helping his father and grandfather work cattle; from an early age he started riding colts and doing a man's work. When Bill was around 12 years old he developed a sore on the inside of one of his knees. It started as a carbuncle, or perhaps a cist; but, due to the fact that Bill was horseback a considerable amount of time, it became inflamed, and infected, and eventually very painful. Jim finally took Bill into Mullen to see the doctor. The doctor examined Bill's sore leg and then paused to visit with Jim, and one of them produced a bottle, and

Top: Bill and Russ Powder River Breaks, Montana, circa 1950.
Bottom: Power River Breaks in eastern Montana, circa 1950. Howell boys hunting prairie chickens.

for a spell Bill and the leg were forgotten while the two men drank and told stories. Finally, almost as and afterthought, the doctor announced that it was time to cut the infected lump off the leg that had been waiting silently on the examination table. "Shall we give it a shot to deaden it, or just cut it off," the doctor asked?

Jim, to which replied, "Just cut it off." Bill, who was one of the most truthful men I ever knew, told me this story 30 years later, and while talking, he stared off into the distance, and gritted his teeth, and said, "And them two /#*/* held me down and cut it off."

In 1948 Jim and Virginia had an opportunity to move to eastern Montana, to the Powder River Breaks, on the east side of the river, 30 miles west of Ekalaka. They bought a ranch there and moved in December, barely getting unloaded before a storm hit dumping a huge amount of snow, which was the start of one of the most severe winters the area had seen in years. In retrospect some people said that Jim made the move to get away from successful in-laws and prove that he could make it on his own. Whatever the reasons, the change was extreme, due mainly to the fact that the Powder River Breaks of eastern Montana were in that day far more primitive than the Sandhills in Nebraska. It was also far colder and the facilities on their new ranch and home were primitive, to say the least, as well as very isolated. There were now six children in the family, and they adapted to the new rugged existence better than their parents: especially Bill, and the second boy, Merle, who was more commonly known as Russ and was four and a half years younger than Bill.

There were always horses: some they owned, others recently traded for, and some being broke for a neighbor. That was the one thing the Howell family soon established in their new neighborhood, a reputation for being able to handle horses. Bill and even Russ were now big enough to handle a green bronc; and by the time Bill was 16 and Russ was 11 or 12, they were capable of running a four- or five-year-old horse that had never been touched into the round corral, and get it saddled, and ridden without any adult supervision.

For awhile Jim had a piece of country leased 9 or 10 miles away from the home place and pastured a small bunch of cows there. In the winter it was Bill's job to ride up there and take care of the cows. He would saddle a bronc, and when it was real cold he would stick his cowboy boots in a water trough and pull them out, and the moisture on the outside of the boots would freeze solid, creating some insulation. He would lope the 10 miles, and hitch up a team, and feed the cattle at the leased place.

The cow market was good when the Howells first moved to Montana, and Jim needed to stock his new ranch. One of his first business decisions was to buy several hundred weaned calves at 40 cents a pound, which was a good price. The plan was to run them until they were 2-year-old steers weighing three times what they did when he bought them. Two years later the bottom fell out of the cow market and Jim sold the steers for 11 cents a pound, which was a financial hit that was hard to recover from. Jim invested in some sheep, and between blizzards, plagues, and hungry coyotes, this also proved to be a bad investment. Mother cows and horses seemed to be the only thing that Jim really had success with.

One day Jim, Bill and Russ gathered a handful of cows and calves and were going to brand. After getting a fire built and the irons getting hot, Jim told Bill to rope. Jim was in an exceptionally good humor and things were going well. After roping about a third of the calves, Bill told Jim that he would be glad to work on the ground and let one of them rope. Jim said that would be fine, and as Bill dismounted and hobbled his horse, Jim told Russ to rope for awhile. Russ was always the carefree one, who wasn't shook-up about anything, and he had forgotten to tie his rope on his saddle when they left camp that morning. Jim had a brand new rope on his saddle that had never been used, and without Jim noticing, Russ walked over and got Jim's rope off his saddle and began roping. After he had roped another third of the calves, Russ suggested to his dad that they trade places, and Jim could finish roping the remaining unbranded calves. Jim walked over and noticed his rope was gone. "Have you boys seen my rope?" he asked.

To which Russ replied, "Yeah, Dad, I borrowed it and it's hanging on my saddle." Jim went into a rage, exuding a torrent of profanity as he cut his new rope into foot long pieces and hurled them as far as his arm could throw them. Bill finished roping the remaining unbranded calves, and everyone knew the good times were over.

When he was 15, Bill started a bronc that had a stronger than average desire to buck. By this time in his life, Bill was capable of fending for himself, including riding colts and other cowboy work. The horse bucked him off repeatedly in spite of his best efforts, and finally, as a last resort, he admitted to Jim that the horse had the best of him. Jim told him he had an idea, and drug out an old pair of heavy Angora chaps and submerged them in a water trough until they were well saturated with water. He told Bill to put on the woollies, get on the outlaw, and see if it was any help. The heavy wet chaps made the difference, and Bill was able to stay on and continued to use the Angora chap treatment for a number of days, finally getting the horse broke.

Bill had quit school at the seventh grade and had been doing a man's work even before that. He literally had grown up making

Bill Howell on bronc at an eastern Montana rodeo, circa 1953.

a hand in some way around horses, cows and even sheep. By the time he was 16 he could handle about anything that was thrown in front of him. Jim was hard to get along with, and the tension between them seemed to escalate until finally there were words said that seemed to point down the long dirt road. Perhaps Jim knew that he needed to fly on his own and deliberately forced his hand, causing Bill to take what few chips he had and leave. At any rate, that's what happened. Bill left home riding the outlaw horse he had conquered with the use of the wooly chaps. Years later his younger brother Harvey, who would have been around six at the time, said that he watched Bill leave, riding the outlaw, and figured Bill must be a man if he could ride away on that horse.

He didn't go very far, probably because he didn't need to. He was well known locally and had the reputation of being able to work hard and get results regardless of the task before him. For awhile he worked for a local man named Jack Hardy running a bulldozer. There were plenty of ranches that needed a good hand. There was a local rancher several years older than Bill named Freeman Peabody, who became a lifelong friend of Bill's. Freeman liked to rope and go to rodeos, and he was getting good at it. Jim Howell was very opposed to rodeos and, for that matter, he was opposed to most everything except work. Bill started hanging out with Freeman and entered the bronc riding at a rodeo or two.

After a few months, Bill decided to go back home and, perhaps, work for Jim awhile. Jim had heard he was coming and was prepared. When Bill rode into the ranch he noticed a big stout horse in the round pole corral but didn't think much of it. He turned his saddle horse loose in the horse pasture after unsaddling him and then went to the house to say hello. Everyone, especially Virginia, was glad to see him and they visited for a short while.

Jim was seated at the kitchen table drinking coffee, and the other boys were sitting around seemingly in anticipation. Jim mentioned that he had heard Bill had been riding a few broncs. Bill answered in the affirmative but said little. "I've got a horse out there in the corral," Jim said and then went on. "I need you to go saddle him and wrangle those horses for me."

It wasn't a request but an order, so Bill left the house and proceeded to the barn. He knew nothing about the horse but could tell by looking at him that he was a mature horse or close to it. It didn't take long to figure out that the horse was unbroke, possibly had never been touched. He knew it was going to be a long day. He had to forefoot the horse, tie him down, and basically start from scratch. Finally, after three or four hours, he got mounted, and turned himself and the bronc loose into the wild blue yonder and somehow got his dad's remuda ran into the corral. Nobody had even come out to watch. Jim was still sitting at the table when he went back and reported that the horses had been gathered. It was obvious that he had no future here, and after visiting a day or two he moved on to whatever lay down the road.

Bill went to work for a man named Glenn Hall who ran cows on several places around Ekalaka. One winter while working for Glenn, Bill was taking care of a couple hundred cows at a cow camp north of town about 10 miles, but he was actually living in town. He would travel out to the cow camp every day where he had a team of work horses that he would hitch to a sled and pull out to a feed ground and feed hay that he had loaded on the sled. A big storm came through the country dumping a lot of snow on the ground, and the road out to the cow camp became impassable due to the deep snowdrifts; and Bill had to ride a horse from town out to camp and back. He would leave in the dark of the morning, and by the time he would get out there, hitch the team up, load the sled with a pitchfork, feed the hay, cut the ice in the spring-fed water trough, and take care of the team, it would be dark again. He would ride home in the dark: it was literally a dark to dark job. After a month of this, the weather finally broke a little, and the road became passable again, and Glenn hired Bill a helper. They were able to get out to the camp in a two-wheel drive pickup (no one had four-wheel drive back then). They had enough time to even stop and have a little lunch, which Bill had not been doing.

There was a little shack at the place, and Bill told his helper that he would cook lunch while the other man chopped ice off the water trough. This arrangement seemed to be working fine for four or five days; and then one day the man burst into the house and announced, "Bill, there ain't no water!" Bill instantly knew what the problem was: the man had only been chopping a small hole in the ice, leaving a lot of ice in the trough, and over a several day period the trough froze solid. It took the two of them all afternoon to chop all the ice out of the trough and get water running again. Bill fired the man, thinking it was better to do things by himself.

Bill got a job running a ranch called the Anderson Place when he was about 19 years old. He wanted to rope and go to some rodeos, so he built a practice arena and started practicing, roping with Freeman Peabody, and once in awhile his brother Russ would show up. The lady he worked for didn't necessarily approve of roping and rodeos and questioned him about the funny looking corral he had built. He parked a tractor the ranch owned in the roping box next to the chute, telling her the little space was specially designed to store equipment. He started going to some rodeos and jackpot ropings and started winning.

People around town started to gossip about Bill being too young to know how to run a ranch. Finally the woman he worked for told Bill that she didn't like people gossiping about her ranch manager. She admitted that under his management the calf crop had increased, as well as the ranch's weaning weights; but she had to fire him anyway because he was just too young—the folks in town all said so.

There was a famous cowboy and rancher in the Ekalaka area who originally came from South Dakota. The man had grown up in the ranching business and had been around horses, including work horses, his whole life. He had a large band of Shire and Thoroughbred mares that had originally been used to raise draft animals, but when he was young he saw the opportunity to raise bucking horses for rodeos. A huge percentage of modern rodeo bucking horses can trace their bloodlines back to that same mare band.

The man's ranch was a few miles north of Jim Howell's ranch in the Powder River Breaks. One time one of the man's employees got bucked off, and the loose saddled horse ran free in the Powder River Breaks for some time because nobody from the man's place could find him. Russ Howell found the horse and caught him, returning him to his owner. The Howells and those people got to know each other, and eventually they paid Bill to break some reject buckers to ride. The fact that Bill could ride them and make saddle horses out of them got on the man's nerves, but the relationship lasted a number of years.

One certain horse that the rancher paid Bill to ride was exceptionally treacherous. The horse was big and full grown

Bill and Gloria in Ekalaka, Montana, circa 1955.

when Bill got him. He wasn't that bad to buck but was real bad on the ground and especially hard to get on. He would come at you, and try to strike you if you were in front of him, or try to jump by you and kick you if you got too far behind your stirrup. Bill had hobbled him, and fore-footed him, and laid him down on numerous occasions, and he finally got where he would stand still if he thought he was hobbled; so whenever Bill wanted to mount or dismount he would throw his rope down, catch his front feet, and pull the rope tight. When he did this the horse would stand and mind his manners.

The horse was nervous and seemed to be thinking of a way to hurt you all the time. He was also hard to bridle. Bill had been riding him in a big heavy bosal; one reason being, he could get that on him easier than a bit. Freeman Peabody had an antique spade bit with a particularly high spoon mouthpiece and cricket. The bit wasn't necessarily a good one but was big and heavy. Freeman gave the bit to Bill and suggested he ride the big outlaw with it, telling him that all that iron in his mouth might give the horse something to think about besides the man trying to ride him. Bill put the spade in the horse's mouth and continued using the heavy rawhide bosal at the same time. It seemed to work: the horse would roll the cricket and slobber, and Bill continued riding him every day and finally got the horse broke, after a fashion, at least. When he returned the horse to his owner and got paid for the breaking job, he warned the fella' that the horse needed to be ridden hard on a steady basis. Bill doubted anyone on the man's place would ride him. Several months later the rancher sent word that the horse was incorrigible and wanted Bill to come and ride him. Bill got to their place and the big horse was in a large pen. The rancher told him they actually hadn't ridden him because they couldn't get the bridle on him. They didn't think Bill could either, beings the horse had been rested for several months. Bill had brought the spade bit with him and walked out into the corral with the bridle in his hand, and when he got to the horse he held the spade bit out like it was a carrot, and the horse laid back his ears and swallowed it, with Bill slipping the headstall on, all in the same quick move.

He saddled him and rode him without incident and then took the spade bit and left. The horse was never ridden again that anyone heard of.

For several years in a row, Bill and Russ got a contract to lamb out 3000 ewes for some people named Glenn and Dale Morgan down toward Alzada. The money was good, and in a month or two the brothers could put together a good stake. Bill took some of the reject buckers off the fellow's place out west of Ekalaka. One time the man who raised the bucking horses was bragging around town about no one being able to ride his horses. Russ told him that it was a bunch of bull because Bill was riding them down at the Morgan Place and had seen him packing lambs in the saddle with him. That didn't set well with the man raising the buckers, and he eventually bet Bill 50 dollars that he couldn't ride one of his good buckers out of a chute at the rodeo grounds in Ekalaka.

The bet was on, and when the day finally came the tension was high. The horse was loaded in the chute, and Bill put a regular stock saddle on him, which was what the bet called for. Bill got down on him, but before he got his right stirrup, someone opened the gate. Bill got the horse rode but never had his right stirrup. The man said he wasn't going to pay off and there was a momentary standoff, and then Russ, who was about 21 years old and no one to mess with, told the rancher, "He does the riding and I do the collecting!" The man got out his checkbook.

The man would go on in the Old Stand Bar in Ekalaka and tell everyone, "I'm going to buck that Howell kid off if it's the last thing I ever do!" He never got it done.

Bill became more interested in roping and traveled around Montana, Wyoming, and the Dakotas roping. He rode a few broncs at first, but what he really enjoyed competing at was roping events. When Russ was old enough, he started going with him, but he was more interested in riding broncs than Bill. At one rodeo, Bill won enough money roping calves to go home to Ekalaka and put a large down payment on a house. At the same time Russ was winning peanuts riding broncs; when he realized Bill was making money, he devoted his rodeo time to roping as well. In 1962 Bill and Russ won the NRCA team tying championship for the year.

There was a roping and rodeo arena on the outskirts of Ekalaka called the 2·20 Club, and they would compete there on a regular basis. They had a few single steer ropings there and Bill competed in that event also. They held an annual 10 steer average steer tripping, and Bill won it at least once.

In 1957 Jim had sold the ranch in the Powder River Breaks, and had moved to town where he bought a house, and ran cows on leased land. You could hear the loudspeaker at the rodeo arena from Jim and Virginia's house, and Bill and Russ's names would be announced as winners on a regular basis, but Jim never mentioned it to them or went down to the arena to watch. He was against nonsense like roping and rodeos.

Bill took a job on a big ranch in northern Utah, and after being there a short time he was made foreman over the cowboy crew. After awhile there was a change in upper management and the Utah job fell apart, but while there he became acquainted with an old cowboy who liked him and wanted to give him advice. He said that Bill had cowboy skills that would be wasted in Montana, but there were some big ranches in Northern Arizona that would appreciate a man like him. He mentioned Babbitts, the Diamond A, and the O RO and told Bill he ought to move south. It seemed like eastern Montana had limited opportunities, and a depressed economy, plus the severely cold winters, so after giving it some thought, he packed up his family and left for the Southwest.

Bill, his wife Gloria, and their two small boys landed in Flagstaff in October of 1963. He was planning on going on to Seligman, but he saw Babbitt Brothers Trading Company signs everywhere and had heard of the big Babbitt Ranch, so he found the Babbitt Ranch office and inquired about a job. He was told to go north 35 miles to a cow camp called Spider Web and talk to Frank Banks. He left Gloria and the boys in town and went to Spider Web and met Frank's wife, Helen, who told him Frank was camped with the cowboy crew at Harbison, 35 miles to the west. As a passing thought, she asked Bill if he would mind delivering a couple of clean shirts to Frank, if he was going to travel out there to ask for a job. Bill took the shirts and left.

He arrived at Harbison while Frank was catching horses for the next day's work, introduced himself, and asked Frank for a job. The conversation was short, Frank answering his request in the negative saying he didn't need anybody, and Bill walked back to his car to leave. When Bill got to his car, he saw the clean shirts, walked back, and handed them to Frank, then turned around to leave a second time. "What kind of horses can you ride?" Frank called after him. Bill turned around and said he was willing to ride whatever kind he needed to ride, to get a job. Frank told him he had some colts and spoiled horses that needed a cowboy on them. Bill said he was interested. They made a deal, and Bill went back to town and found a place for his family to live, then took his bed and saddle back out to the CO Bar wagon.

The outfit had lots of young horses, and more than a few that had been ridden enough to have lost their fear of man, and rested enough to be fresh. Bill had found a place he could shine, because at 29 years of age he had way more experience with rank horses than most. He also had enough fear of starvation in him to work harder than most. Frank Banks liked him and offered him a steady job as a camp man when the fall roundup ended six weeks or so after Bill was hired on. He moved his wife Gloria and two sons into Redlands, 80 miles northwest of Flagstaff. After a few months, Frank promoted Bill into a foreman position on the W Triangle Ranch, and more and more Frank let Bill run the crew without his interference. When Bill had worked for Frank about a year and a half, Frank ran onto a neighboring rancher named Claude Neal and told him he had found a man whom he was going to train to take his place. Frank gave Bill more responsibility, including installing a considerable amount of new pipeline to parts of the ranch that were short of water.

In 1967 Frank told Bill that he had plans to retire and wanted him to take his place. Bill answered him, expressing his doubts that he was capable of doing the job; to which Frank candidly replied in agreement, but Frank went on to say that he was willing to teach Bill if he would continue working for him a couple years. Frank moved Bill to the CO Bar so Bill could learn the country and the operation over there. In doing so he became the jigger boss there, the same as he had been on the W Triangle.

Fall roundup at Babbitts would start soon after Labor Day weekend and would continue pretty much nonstop until sometime in December. The cowboy crew, under Frank's management, would go back and forth between the W Triangle and the CO Bar, and though the two ranches were two separate blocks of land, with neighbors owning country in between the two, for all practical purposes were managed like one unit. Fall shipments were usually made in November, but there was lots of other cow work to be done, weaning, moving cattle from summer to winter pastures, etc.

Trailing Babbitt cattle.

There is a camp on the CO Bar called Aso (pronounced Ā·so), which consists of a set of weaning corrals, and several holding traps, as well as a small shack or camp house. Around the first of December in 1967, Frank, Bill, and all the cowboy crew weaned a large bunch of calves at Aso and turned them out in a trap, intending to leave them there until they quit bawling and acting stressed.

By that time of year, most of the cow work would be in the lower country, or winter range, and the crew was camped at

Spider Web 15 miles northeast of Aso. Frank and Bill's families also lived there: Spider Web being like a headquarters, especially in the wintertime.

On the thirteenth of December, it began to snow and continued to do so for four days, nonstop. By the time the storm finally broke and passed on to the east, it had virtually crippled a great deal of Arizona and the Southwest. There was over three feet of snow on the level at Spider Web and seven feet in Flagstaff. Many parts of the CO Bar and W Triangle had four feet and more. There wasn't a single four-wheel drive vehicle on the ranch and no heavy equipment. It was anybody's guess where and how far cattle had drifted, or if they were surviving at all.

Frank's immediate concern was the freshly weaned calves at Aso; he ordered a Bulldozer from somewhere to be shipped out to the ranch, as well as several loads of hay. He also called the Ford garage in Flagstaff and bought the first four-wheel drive truck the ranch ever owned. As soon as the rented dozer arrived, he had the Cat skinner blade a trail up the hill to Aso and sent Bill and four men with two horses apiece to camp in the line shack there.

They arrived at Aso late in the day and had enough groceries and hay to last a day or two. They were hoping to make short work out of gathering the calves and starting them down the Cat track to Spider Web. From Spider Web looking toward Aso and the San Francisco Peaks, which are over 12 thousand feet high and 25 miles away, all you see is the north slope of extinct volcanoes and mountains. The country rises in elevation as you go south. Aso, the camp itself, sits in a shallow draw amidst several basalt, or malpai, hills, all of which are old volcanoes. The trap where the calves had been turned out is on the south side of the corrals and campsite, and there are two large hills inside its boundaries. The hill directly south of the camp rises at least 600 feet in elevation, and the top of the hill is about a mile from the small shack. Everything rises looking toward the hill, and the snow at Aso was about four feet on the level; and on the north slopes, which is what most of the holding trap consisted of, were drifts much deeper. Looking up across the white abyss to the top of the hill, it appeared like most of the calves in the trap had walked to the very peak and were stranded there. There were between 1200 and 1500 of them.

Early in the morning, after spending a short and cold night in the old line shack, the men saddled up and started their struggle up the hill. They managed to ride a great deal of the first three-quarters of a mile, their horses managing to break a trail through the deep crusted snow. The last 300 yards, the snow, which had drifted, became much deeper in places; and the incline eventually increased to 50 degrees. Sometimes the snow was chest high, and the men would take turns walking and struggling to break a trail. It was bitter cold and the summit seemed forever out of reach. They finally climbed out on top about midday, and to their astonishment, they looked and saw that the south slope of this very steep hill was completely bare of snow. The prevailing winds had come out of the southwest and they had blown the slope clean. Their view had been nothing but north slopes and continuous deep snow. Going down was easy compared to what they had been through all morning.

One of the men in the crew was named Joe Chavez, and he was often very difficult to get along with. The two horses Joe had chosen to ride while rescuing the Aso calves looked just alike. One of them was humpy and Joe was afraid of him, while the other was quite gentle. The day after gathering the calves, they started them down the bulldozed trail, and Joe was riding the gentle horse. At midday they changed horses, and Joe unsaddled the gentle one and turned him loose. A minute later he caught the same gentle horse and saddled him up and stepped on. An hour later he suddenly started cursing and exclaimed that he was riding the same horse. He questioned Bill, asking him why he hadn't told him he had caught the same horse. "I figured you were afraid to ride the other one!" Bill told him. "You've been riding them both all fall. I had no idea you couldn't tell them apart." Joe was bowed up for a month.

There is an old saying among cowboys, "Being a jigger boss, or second in command, amounts to nothing more than being a pissing post." A jigger can be given a lot of responsibility but given very little room to make decisions. If things go well, the wagon boss can take all the credit, and if they go badly, the jigger might get the blame even if he really doesn't deserve it. It goes with the territory; if you don't like it, don't be a jigger. Actually, Bill had the utmost respect for Frank and never, even in old age, failed to recognize Frank as a mentor and a friend. Still, there was a time or two that being second in command seemed less than worth it. Every boss has favorites, or men in the crew whom others think get all the glory and cream. There was an old Texan named Rufus Wynn who seemed to be Frank's favorite. Rufe held a certain amount of resentment toward Bill, probably because he could see the changing of the guard coming ,and he wasn't looking forward to it. Bill had been running the branding wagon for Frank who hadn't been around much. The wagon was camped at Cedar Ranch, and Bill and his family were living there also. One evening Bill was sitting down with his family to eat supper after a hard day of branding. Frank knocked on the door and entered the kitchen while everyone was sitting at the table eating. Frank declared, "Bill, Rufe tells me that you haven't been taking turns dragging calves." It was as much a question as a statement.

Bill had had his fill of being jigger and Rufe talking trash behind his back, and he jumped up and loudly exclaimed, "What do you think, Frank?"

Frank backed up and said, "By golly, I think you have been, Bill. I think you have been!" Nothing more was said about not taking turns roping.

Frank retired in June of 1969 and turned the management over to Bill. It was a hard act to follow, but Frank had picked and trained Bill himself and they parted on the best of terms. Frank would come up and visit and just hang out for years to come. But there were several men who just couldn't accept the new man, especially old Rufe. Bill thought Rufe was a great cowboy but the change was too much. Not many days after Frank left, Rufus called a friend, who was much younger, and who shared a mutual hatred for Bill. The hombre was big and had a reputation of being the toughest man in Coconino County. He drove into Spider Web late in the afternoon, and Bill was in the kitchen of the bunkhouse washing dishes for the cook. There were no other men around besides Bill, Rufus, and the notorious tough guy who entered the kitchen with Rufus close behind, smiling. "I don't think you can run this outfit, Bill, and I don't think you can whip me either!" the hombre said. He was 7 inches taller and 50 pounds heavier and stood a few feet in front of the door connecting the kitchen and bedroom, squeezed into a small space between the kitchen table and refrigerator. Bill stood in the middle of the room six feet away and waited. After a minute or two the bad man turned around and left with Rufus in tow. Rufe never came back.

Bill was now the big boss of a very big ranch with a very large history, and the shadow of Frank would be slow in dispersing. Frank's prowess as a man was legendary, and he could drink whiskey like a man with prowess should: or so many whiskey drinkers thought. There were many cowboys who had been in Arizona a long time and who couldn't have packed pigging strings for Frank, but liked to claim friendship, especially in the midst of a saloon, and who resented the man from Montana getting Frank's job, regardless of how good a bronc rider he might be. It would be awhile before Bill was as accepted as he eventually was. When I first heard of Bill, he had been running the Babbitt Ranch for over a year. The first conversation I overheard about Bill was issuing forth from a well-known Arizona cowboy talking about the Babbitt Ranch being short-handed because the good hands didn't like working for the Montanan who didn't know how to work cattle the Arizona way, whatever that was supposed to be. I was as green as May in Ireland, but I thought I detected a hint of jealousy, and even hope that the man wouldn't last long as Babbitt wagon boss.

Jim Howell rode a slick fork saddle and roped with a tied rope and was left-handed. When Bill landed in Arizona, he was still riding a slick fork saddle with about a three inch cantle, the kind he had been raised in. In spite of the lack of swells, he had proved he could ride any horse someone ran under him. He was

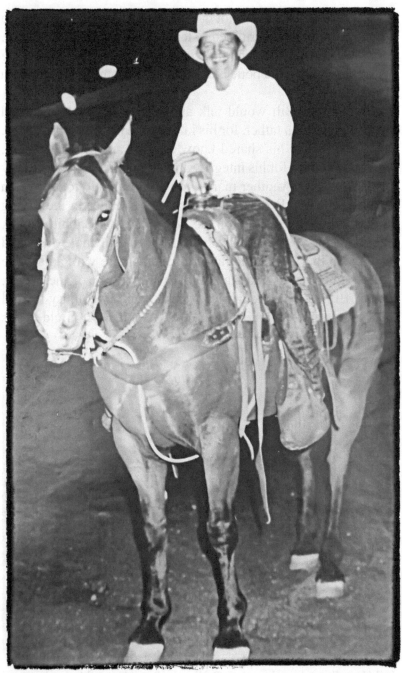

Ben Fancher on his famous rope horse Yaqui. Photo courtesy Jim Fancher.

an expert roper but could not dally, and sometime after going to work for Frank he determined to learn. Dallying on a slick horn, he forced himself to adapt and years later would tell of burning his hands clean to the bone before finally becoming proficient in his new craft.

When old, Bill would talk about several people who had mentored him: his father, for his knowledge of cattle and horses; Frank Banks, for his shared knowledge of ranch management; and John Babbitt, for his integrity and giving him the opportunity to run the outfit. Another man who was a big help to Bill when he needed it was Ben Fancher. Ben was a leader in the roving band of men who worked on the places like the Babbitt Ranch. Ben went to work for Bill not long after Bill took over, and recognized that he was not an ordinary hombre with a hat. The two became friends and stayed that way the rest of their lives. One of Bill's greatest qualities was his lack of jealousy toward men who might be his equal in cowboy skills. He could be, as

Bill Howell catching horses at Redlands, Boog Howell in background. Photo by Kurt Markus.

I later found out, very difficult to be around at times; but he was never jealous or deceitful toward a man who had skills comparable to, or even exceeding, his own. He wasn't afraid of someone who might outrope or outride him, and eventually that quality began to pay off, and good young cowboys started showing up wanting a job.

I showed up at Cedar Ranch on May 11, 1974, and asked Bill for a job. He was cooking for the crew, beings the outfit was temporarily out of a man who had those skills. He offered me a cooking job or a cowboy job, telling me he had one untaken mount of horses left in the remuda. I figured I could ride better than cook so I took the horses. It was a Friday, and at noon someone wrangled, and Bill roped me two horses that were barefoot and told me to shoe them, and then everyone was going to get the weekend off.

The first horse he roped and led out to me was a bay horse with a star and a snip, and he told me his name was Polecat. As I slipped his rope off Polecat's neck and my bridle on, he said in a matter-of-fact tone, "This horse is going to buck and you darn sure better not pull on his head!" I took that to mean that he might fall over backwards if much pressure was applied to the bridle reins when he was bucking but couldn't help but wonder if there was a company rule about not pulling one's head up. He turned around and took several steps, building another loop in his rope, and then turned and looked at me and Polecat, who were standing close together, "What a miserable */+^#*/. I hoped he was talking about Polecat and not me.

On Monday morning we saddled up just before sunup, and Bill instructed Harvey Howell, nicknamed Boog, who was the jigger boss, to load everyone up in a bobtail horse truck and haul a short distance to the backside of the Cedar Ranch horse pasture and make a drive in S P Pasture. When we got loaded, Boog told me that we were hauling out because Bill thought it might uncock Polecat a little and keep him from flipping over backwards. The distance was short, and soon I was slipping up on the beast as everyone waited to see if the newcomer was going to stay on. It was evident that everyone expected action to be unavoidable. I figured the best way to win a fight was throw the first punch, so I tried to drive a spur rowel into Polecat's right lung and the first of many duels began. I followed orders and had my right fist gripping a night latch and threw plenty of slack in the bridle reins. I was thankful for the warning because the first jump was as close to straight up and down as I care to be, but after a jump or two he took his head and farted off in a straight line. I lost count of how many times the horse blew up and tried to get rid of me, and by the end of the day I had all the bronc riding practice I wanted. Luckily, I never fell off.

We made a drive to the northwest corner of SP pasture next to the Tub's horse pasture and paired out about 100 pair and stuck them through the fence into Mesa Butte pasture. We trailed the 100 pair to Mesa Butte storage four miles away, and Bill showed up in a pickup with the branding outfit and his three boys: Vic, Tim, and Tom, who were about 12, 11, and 10 years old, respectfully. I was impressed with the boys, who were obviously experienced helping in the branding pen and conducted themselves like little men. Halfway through the branding, Boog told me to take a turn dragging calves, and I managed to rope a few. We were done by 10:30 in the morning.

When we got back to Cedar Ranch, we discovered that Mike Lenton, the old one-eyed maintenance man, who had been working for the outfit 40 years, had been to town and retrieved an alcoholic short-order cook named Lee, who was our new roundup cook. Lee had the delirium trembles so badly he could mix pancakes or bread dough with ease. If he could manage to clutch the mixing bowl to his bosom with a tight hold, and stab a large spoon into its cavity, the DT's would take over and soon the ingredients were mixed to a fine puree.

Beings we now had a cook, Bill was freed up to ride, and the next morning we made another drive in the SP and paired out 99 pair and corralled them at SP tank. Bill was riding a good looking bay horse named Coon, who stood about 14.3 and might have weighed 1075 or 1100 if real fat. We drove into the northeast corner of SP and started pairing out. As the cattle came trailing out of the corner of the pasture we started letting any pair that was straight go by and holding anything that wasn't mothered up. As the cattle went by us paired out they could keep going and pass through an open gate into a large water lot surrounding a very large dirt tank. The first 75 pair went by within a few minutes with Bill and I being in the front doing most of the ducking and dodging, which was great fun. Finally the herd got stopped, and Bill sent Boog into the herd to start

Bill Schoolin' on Coon - *by Mike Capron*

cutting pairs out one at a time. Things were moving real fast, and we were never at rest more than a second or two as the cattle were fat and feeling good, and had been worked this way enough that they knew the program and wanted to keep moving by us. A cow with two calves came at Bill and me, and we gave her a little ground trying to figure out which of the two calves belonged to the cow. Bill jumped Coon to the right to turn another cow that was trying to make a break, but had his head turned around to the left watching the cow and two calves between us, and as this was happening, Coon felt the man a little off balance and blew up and went to bucking. The first jump was high and fast and Bill's fanny came about 18 inches out of the saddle and he lost his right stirrup. The second jump he got himself sucked back down, and stirrup or no stirrup, Coon got fed a considerable amount of iron.

We paired out exactly 99 pair and put them in a branding pen and Bill took a turn roping, which I was told he had not done in a long while. He roped all 99 calves, and I watched him like a hawk, and he never missed a loop. I've heard John Cline, who was a famous Arizona cowboy, had a standing bet that he could heel 100 calves anytime without missing. I've heard other people say they could do it, but that was the only time I witnessed someone roping that many without missing at least once. He did it riding a horse most cowboys couldn't have ridden.

The CO Bar went as far to the east as the Little Colorado River between Wupatki National Monument and Cameron, and west of the river 50 miles. It also went north as far as the Kaibab Forest near the Grand Canyon and then south around the west slope of the San Francisco Peaks, almost all the way to Bellemont. The cowboy crew trailed cattle toward the river and 5000 feet elevation in the winter, and then uphill to summer at 8000 feet or higher. We were constantly trailing cows somewhere.

Arizona is famous for its cowboys who are experts at the art of gathering wild cattle, and rightly so. Although most don't know it, there is an art to gathering large herds of gentle cattle also. A large herd of cows with big weaner calves, say about 1500 pair, can be lost just as easily as a dozen mavericks in the

Hualapais if not handled correctly. Moving cows and small baby calves over long distances can be as big a wreck as you can find anywhere. I've seen and heard of crews moving big bunches of cows and babies where the entire crew was walking behind the herd with tin cans full of rocks making noise, trying to keep the calves going, none of them knowing where their mothers were. I never witnessed that at Babbitts. Bill was a master at handling large numbers of cattle. Everything he did was for the welfare of the cow and giving her a chance to raise her calf.

Bill had a memory for a cow that was legendary. When I went to work for Babbitts, they had about 4200 mother cows on the W Triangle and CO Bar combined, all of them horned Hereford cows. Numerous times I've seen Bill question a cowboy about a certain cow. Perhaps it was a tight-bagged cow walking the fence trying to get back to where she had last seen her calf, or perhaps it was a cow that needed doctored or given a little attention. "What did she look like?" he would ask.

"Well, she was a Hereford cow." the man might reply.

"Yeah, but what did she look like?" he would ask again. He figured you ought to know. The fact that 4000 horned Hereford cows look the same to most people didn't make sense to him; he could tell them apart.

In the fall we would throw big herds together and work them, sometimes as many as 1500 cows plus their calves and bulls. When Bill rode into a herd of cattle to start cutting, he knew what he was looking for. He was constantly moving in a big herd. I've seen men stop in a large herd of cattle and gaze slowly around acting like they were pondering their navels or what the cook was going to cook for supper. He believed, if you wanted to find a certain cow to cut out, you moved until you found her. Then you cut her out, and entered the herd, and moved again. Many times I've seen him have two separate cuts outside of a big herd. Possibly one cut would be nothing but dry cows, and the other would be cull cows that had sucking calves. At least once I saw him position three separate cuts outside a large herd we were working near the Tubs camp. If you were between the roundup and the cuts, and he brought a critter out to the edge and cut her by you, he expected you to be cowman enough to know which of the cuts she should run into. He was constantly making you think. You were constantly given the opportunity to practice your cowboy skills or use your knowledge of a cow. He did not want to have to explain it to you; he wanted you to figure it out yourself. If you couldn't get it figured out, he would move you to the backside where you weren't required to know anything. If you didn't improve, you would eventually

Bill Howell dragging calves at the CO Bar Ranch. Photo by Kurt Markus

get moved plumb off the outfit. If a critter ran off trying to get away, he wanted you to rope it, the faster the better. If a horse bucked and you could remove some of his hair while riding him, that was fine with him. He worked fast, too fast for some men who would complain about him being wild and hard on cattle. Actually, they were complaining because they couldn't keep up with him. He was the most conscientious man about the welfare of cattle I ever saw, but he did not believe in being slow or that screwing around benefited the cow or anybody. Get it done, and do it like a cowboy, and let's move on because we've got plenty to do somewhere else, was the constant theme.

It has been said that you can have your own opinion, but you cannot have your own facts. Here are some interesting facts, leaving opinion aside. When Bill took over as Babbitt Ranch manager, the ranch had one of the premier herds of Hereford cows in America. In the twenty-two and a half years Bill ran the outfit, the shipping weights of Babbitt yearlings increased by 150 pounds. In the 15 years I was around the outfit, the calf crop was never lower than 82 percent, with the average over time being 85 percent; and several years the calf crop on the W Triangle was in the 90s, and once 98 percent. Bill branded, while managing, somewhere around 75 thousand calves and never used a calf table. In the 15 years I was present as a witness, we shipped somewhere around 45 thousand yearlings and 75 hundred cull cows and never once had to cancel a shipping because we weren't ready and waiting for the trucks to arrive. The ranch grazed cattle on vast pastures of federal land and was never in violation or threatened with trespass due to being in a pasture at the wrong time or overgrazing. A continuous maintenance program was in place, and ranch infrastructure, such as fencing, watering facilities, etc., was as good or better at the end of his tenure as the beginning. When he took over in 1969 the outfit had the reputation as having the hardest to ride, buckingest remuda in the southwest; a few years after Bill retired the ranch won the AQHA Bayer Ranch Remuda of the Year award. The first good Driftwood stud, which really turned the Babbitt horse program around, was bought by Bill the first winter I worked for him. In 15 years I never saw him get bucked off and I saw him ride lots of buckers. I never heard of Babbitts, or Bill, cheating an employee out of a day's wages, and I never knew of a neighbor calling Bill a thief. I never once heard Bill speak disrespectfully about his boss, John Babbitt; and though he would laugh and tell stories about some of his and Frank Banks' misunderstandings, he always spoke very highly of Frank and gave him credit for giving him the chance to excel. In the fifteen years I worked for Bill, I had to work after sundown one time. That's not saying he was perfect, because he had a few peculiarities.

I spent the summer of 1974 at Redlands, and then right after Labor Day we went to work. It was dry over a lot of the ranch that summer, especially the CO Bar winter country. We trailed cows down east of the highway at Wupatki, and then across to Bardoni well, and it was the saddest sight you ever saw with very little feed to winter on. Bill commented to me years later that it was a stressful time, worrying about how we were going to make it through the winter on such short grass. They put out lots of cake that winter on the CO Bar, but I spent December and January at Redlands where feed conditions were quite a bit better.

On the first of January, I gathered two coming five-year-old geldings to break to ride. They were out of Frank Banks' mare band: one being a solid sorrel I named Paycheck, and a red roan I named Red Bluff. They had Frank's U7 brand on them. The night I gathered them there came a big snow about 18 inches on the level at Redlands. It snowed hard from about sundown

Ed Ashurst necking calves out of a roundup, outside branding, CO Bar Ranch, circa 1981.

Bill Howell necking calves out of a roundup outside, no corral.

until sometime early in the morning, but by sunup it had cleared off and was quite a ways below zero. I was nervous and didn't want to lay around, so Pat Cain and I saddled up and roped the broncs around the neck and then fore-footed them and tied them down. I then hobbled them front and behind and let them up. I then sacked them out, saddled them and rode them. By the time I got on the first one, the snow in the corral was packed down to a hard five to six inches. They were pretty wary of the slick ground and didn't buck. By the first of February they were going pretty good, and I could run and rope a cow and make them look like they knew what they were doing.

The first of February, Bill moved me back to Spider Web to start the early works there. We gathered all the cows that were turned out in what they call Southside and cut out about 1200 to trail out to the Knobs, 25 miles to the west. Getting this herd gathered and ready to go took three or four days, and when we had the ones Bill wanted, we put them in the Three-Cornered trap a mile west of Spider Web. We were going to trail them to SP tank 15 miles west the next day. That night it snowed at least a foot at Spider Web and maybe a couple inches more several miles west.

When we got up in the morning it was foggy but very cold, probably around zero. Nobody was relishing the day ahead, looking at 1200 hungry cow's behinds as they walked slowly west for 15 miles. I wondered if maybe Bill would postpone things for a day. I had only been around for nine months, so I didn't know him well. We saddled up before sunup. I was riding Red Bluff and had on so many clothes I could barely get on. When I got on he tried to buck me off, but I had so many clothes on he couldn't throw that much weight off. Bill's boys, Vic, Tim, and Tom, were helping us. Vic was maybe 13 and Tom, the youngest, was 11. I watched them and thought, if they can do this, surely I can. The sun never came out all day and it never got above 20. Tom and I were close together all day, and I remember we would get off and walk to keep our feet warm. It was cold! There was no feed where these cattle came from and, cold or no cold, they needed to be moved somewhere where they had a chance of surviving. The second day it snowed again, blowing little pea-sized ice balls straight into our faces for several hours. It took us three days to get the cattle to Dent and Sayer where we turned them loose.

I marveled at Bill's boys and how they worked like men in such adverse conditions. It was apparent to me that he cared for them very deeply, but didn't treat them like little kids. He talked

Ed Ashurst and Ben Fancher, Mormon Lake, 1976.

to them like they were men. They worked with a crew of men and knew how to interact with men. You felt safe around them, never having the feeling that they were going to run and tell Daddy if you did something Bill wouldn't approve of. They were exceptional hands for their ages, obviously being the recipients of some good private tutelage of all things cowboy. You never got the feeling that Bill was protecting them, and it appeared they had free rein to find their own boundaries.

The fall of 1976 started out like any other and things went smoothly until around the first of November. We shipped cull cows on the CO Bar around the last day of October and then moved to Tin House on the W Triangle side where there had been a crew gathering yearlings. We arrived, and Bill's right hand man on that side told him they were short lots of yearlings, especially heifers. They seemed to have vanished, or so was the report.

Bill went driving around and found dried out heifers in a fence corner on the Diamond A side of the fence. A big bunch of about 35 had gotten out into Broken Axle pasture on the Diamond A where there was no water, and had drifted east, and had hung up in a corner, and were dying of thirst. As Bill drove up in a truck he could see several dead heifers on the Diamond A, and fresh horse tracks on the Babbitt side of the fence. He opened the gate and let the ones that were still alive drift through and start walking toward water. The steers we were short were found in the Tom Moore pasture and were finally all accounted for. Things were tense around camp for a day or two, as it was evident that too much alcohol had prevented some people from doing their best.

We gathered Tom Moore pasture and put that bunch of cattle into a trap between Rogers tank and the Tom Moore fence, about four or five miles east of Tin House. The next day Bill sent me to trail the herd of cows and calves to Tin House, and then after lunch we would wean the calves. There were about 350 cows, almost all of which had big calves on their side, plus around 17 bulls. We gathered the trap without incident and let them out a gate about a quarter mile east of Rogers tank. As the cattle drifted through the gate, Joe Chaves rode through after the first 40 or 50 cows and turned them toward camp, which could be seen probably four and a half miles away.

After the last cow had walked through the gate, everything was going fine, beings Joe had them turned toward camp and the cattle were traveling along just right. Joe, in the process of all this, had positioned himself on the left point, which was not what I envisioned because he did not tend to do a good job as a point man. But he was 25 years older than me, and I didn't want to be disrespectful to him by riding up and replacing him, so I stayed where I had ended up after coming through the gate. Bill Van Praag was on the right point, which was good because he was a top hand. Between Bill Van Praag and me was another cowboy named Jim, who was 25 years my senior and supposed to be a good hand. Cisco Scott was there on my left and three or four other men whom I can't remember.

Things were going smoothly for a mile or so, but slowly Joe let the left point widen out, and cattle on his side were grazing as much as walking and it was slowing us down, but I held my peace, thinking it would be better to muck my way through it rather than make an older man mad because I, a boy of 25, had told him how to point a herd. Joe was famous for doing things like this just to stir up trouble.

Pretty soon, Jim, the man in front of me, quit doing anything except riding in a slow walk way out to the side and acting bowed up. Before too long the cattle on the right flank, where Jim was riding, widened out because of his lack of effort, and many started to graze. I thought about riding in front of him and whipping the herd back into shape, but that would have gone against cowboy manners, and I did not want to insult an older man.

Joe Chaves could tell his efforts to cause trouble were succeeding, and he widened out farther on the left point and cattle on that side completely stopped walking. Someone on my left stopped and dismounted, acting like he needed to adjust his saddle, and then someone else followed suit. Bill Van Praag, who was on the right point and was my closest friend (he would be the best man at my wedding three months later) rode off to a hill a quarter mile away and unsaddled his horse. Slowly the herd came to a complete stop and started to fan out, especially to the right, because of the absence of Bill Van Praag and buckaroo Jim's lack of effort. He had dismounted and was sulking.

The herd had widened out on both sides for 300 yards and all the cattle were grazing. The grass was good due to ample summer rains in the area. Things were peaceful for about 15 minutes, and I pondered my predicament, which basically was a case of mutiny, resulting from a lack of respect on some men's parts and a lack of leadership on mine. And then a calf, which was full of grass, but separated from his mother, picked its head up and bawled. Its mother did not respond because the calf had been sucking her for six or eight months and was about weaned anyway. It was the time of year that cows don't tend to babies nearly as much as they would if the calf was a month old. The calf weighed 600 pounds, and the cow was content to graze. Then another calf bawled and looked around for a moment and put its head back down to graze a little more. And then another and another, and in a matter of five minutes there were 50 or 60 big fat calves bawling, and they were all starting to turn east, which was the direction their confused minds remembered last seeing their mothers.

I wasn't the greatest cowboy on the planet, but I could tell we were fixing to have a full scale wreck that would set the roundup back by at least one day. Bill Howell would write down a schedule in a yellow legal pad and would predict what we would be doing two or three months in advance. He was a man who liked things clicking like a well-oiled clock, and he had entrusted me with a day in his legal pad that had been written down ten weeks earlier. In my mind I knew that in a minute a calf was going to make a break, and someone in the crew would pursue it, and things would snowball, and the herd would be lost.

I stepped on my horse, and in a split second he was in a dead run with me screaming at the top of my lungs and slapping my heavy shotgun chaps with my bridle reins, and I went to moving the cattle myself. I raced and screamed and shook things up considerably, and in a minute the herd went to shaping up, and Cisco and a couple other young guys got on and followed suit, and the cows bawled in excitement and found their calves, and we got them strung out and moving again. Old Joe Chaves saw that his attempt to cause a wreck and make me look like a fool had failed, and he even started making a hand.

I loped out to the hill where Bill Van Praag was and asked him to help me. He replied that he figured everyone was mad at him for some reason so he had rode off. I explained that Joe was a trouble causer, and Jim was a conceited ass, but nobody was mad at him. He said fine and mounted up and took his place on the right point.

I ended up directly behind Bill Van Praag, where my buckaroo Jim had originally been. He was now in my place, and riding along bowed up, and acting like a seven-year-old even though he was 52. After a minute or so, I rode up to Buckaroo Jim and apologized to him for riding around him, saying I had to do something or I was going to lose the herd for sure. He cursed me and said he didn't give a damn, and he was going to quit this sorry */^#* outfit anyway. I told him he was telling the wrong man because I didn't have a company checkbook, but Bill did, and he could take off and lope to camp and tell Bill, who would be waiting there. He didn't reply but continued to ride along helping in no way and looking angry, so I ignored him. When we got to camp with the herd, he didn't quit but, in fact, worked for the outfit for about seven more years.

Every fall Buckaroo Jim would get in a fight with someone, and it would always start over his opinion about trailing cattle. Two years later he got in a screaming match with a man the same age as him, who, in fact, was superior to him as a cowboy. Before the screaming match ended, they both swore they were going to get their guns and start shooting.

The best cow horse I ever saw was a Babbitt horse that Bill broke and trained himself. I never saw or heard of anyone else riding him. The horse was out of a stud called Clabber, who was supposed to be a colt by the famous stallion of the same name. The original Clabber was by My Texas Dandy and a mare named

Blondie S. In 1938 A.B. Nichols of Gilbert, Arizona, went to Texas and purchased the original Clabber when the stud was a two-year-old. A.B. Nichols' son, Buck, who was a close friend of Bill's, said that the Babbitt Clabber horses did not resemble the original Clabber at all. The original Clabber was bred to run and produced 1 world champion, 27 Racing Registers of Merit, and 52 race starters. He was a very clean-made horse; whereas, the Babbitt Clabber horses tended to be feather-legged and thick in the neck. That being said, the Babbitt Clabbers were good horses when you got one broke, which wasn't easy because a lot of them bucked.

Bill called his famous cutting horse Checkers, and he was about ten years old when I first saw him. Checkers was a big streak-faced chestnut sorrel that stood 15 hands and weighed around 1200, give or take a little. Bill didn't ride the horse much and usually wouldn't shoe him except in the fall when he would use him a few times when he had a big herd to work and lots of cutting to do. I personally never saw anything to compare with him. If we had a large herd thrown together, sometimes 1200 or 1300 head, Bill wanted the cattle spread out, which would make it easier to find and keep pairs together. A horse must travel and move a great distance if you cut out several hundred head over a several hour period. I never saw Checkers get tired, or act like he was out of gas, and would look like he was trying just as hard after cutting several hundred cattle as he had when he cut the first. The horse seemed to understand pairs and would watch a cow and her calf at the same time. People talk about horses that a cow can't get away from, and Checkers' claim is closer to fitting that description than any other horse I've seen. He worked straight up, with his head usually elevated, with nose tucked; he did not lean sideways in the style of the show cutters, but he would get his butt in the ground and turn back as pretty as anything I ever witnessed. When looking at a cow, he usually had one ear forward and one turned back. I never saw Bill make the horse slide or spin or demonstrate his prowess as a reiner. I did hear Bill make a comment once saying, "I've been working cattle for 50 years, and I've never needed a horse to spin."

Bill and Checkers Doing What They Do Best - *by Mike Capron*

I saw Bill and Checkers do something once that was unlike anything I ever saw. We were going to ship cull cows at Spider Web, either the fall of 1975 or '76, and we had stripped the calves off a bunch of old cows that were going to be sold. We put the calves in the alley, and Bill wanted to separate the steers from the heifers. We had plenty of help, and he could have put a man in a gate and ducked one sex in the gate and let the others by. Instead, he told Boog and me to go down to the other end of the alley and push the calves toward him, and he stayed at the opposite end, in front of an open gate. I thought it odd to be doing it this way and figured it was best to be real easy and not push the calves fast or hard, and Boog seemed to be thinking the same thing. We were deliberately going slow, and he let a calf or two by, and all of a sudden he hollered and gave Boog and me a good cussing, telling us to get the lead out and put the calves to him. "Alright, you arrogant big shot." I thought to myself, "You're fixing to get a bunch of calves shoved down your throat!" I went to whipping and spurring, and I can get a bunch of calves going when I want, and pretty soon the calves were stacked up in front of Bill, and they were sure wanting to go somewhere. Bill spurred and jerked on Checkers' bridle reins one time, and the horse went to ducking and diving, and the darndest bunch of sorting took place I ever saw. Boog and I continued to whip and spur, forcing him to make a mistake. At one point I actually saw Checkers reach down between his front legs, and bite a calf, and toss it out in front of him. The entire process took perhaps one minute and there were 75 calves through the open gate and 75 calves in the alley. "I surrender," I thought to myself. But Bill said nothing; instead, he turned around and rode off to conquer the next thing that was on his agenda.

Bill could be a great deal of fun around a crew when he was in a good humor and not stressed about something. He was an excellent storyteller and had an unlimited amount of them to tell if you could get him to start talking. He also loved a good storyteller. One fall we had a buckaroo from Nevada working with us named Kent Craven. Kent was a storyteller, a superb spinner-of-yarns, who knew how to turn it on when he had a captive audience. Late in the fall we were camped at Redlands, and one night Kent got to telling stories about various escapades he had witnessed in his travels, and beings he was in high form we were all listening and laughing. At the punch line of one particularly outrageous tale, I saw Bill on the floor, on his hand and knees, pounding his fists in glee, he was enjoying himself so much.

If he was in the mood, and around people he liked, Bill was no party pooper, but he had no patience for people he thought were acting stupidly. One spring in the late '80s, we were camped at Cedar Ranch branding calves. It was June and hot and dry. Early one morning while we were eating breakfast, a young man, about 25 years old, drove into camp in a Toyota pickup and asked directions to somewhere. We answered his questions and then he went on his way. Late that afternoon Bill and Vic Howell, and I were going to Spider Web where our families lived, and we were going to return to the wagon early the next morning. As we drove by SP tank, which is about halfway to Spider Web, we passed the Toyota pickup we had seen early that morning but saw no one around it. Thinking nothing of it, we drove on. When we got down the road another six miles, we saw the young man walking ahead of us in the direction of Highway 89, the same as us. He was within 100 yards of a 1200 gallon water trough on a pipeline. The trough was full of water. Vic was driving, I was in the middle, and Bill was sitting by the passenger door. "Pull up there and stop and we'll see what this pilgrim is doing, Vic." Bill ordered. And when we got next to the young man Bill rolled down his window. The young man looked fine to me and seemed to be walking along like a normal healthy young 25-year-old.

Before Bill could inquire about the young man's needs, the boy blurted out in as theatrical a style as he could muster, "Water!" his voice cracking in feigned desperation, and he held out an empty hand in our direction as if we were going to hand him a flask of cool spring-fed liquid.

"You stupid son of a gun *#/^#/*, get your stupid *#/^#* backside in the back of the truck!" The boy looked at the three of us in shock at our lack of concern over his condition, which he figured was near death. "Get in, you stupid *#/^#/*!" And with that Bill rolled up his window, and for a minute the boy stood there staring. When he saw Vic put it in drive, he hopped in the back and we sped down the road. "Take this pilgrim down to Hank's Trading Post and dump him out!" Bill ordered Vic. Ten minutes later we pulled into the trading post, which was on Highway 89, and he was instructed to get out, and then we drove off and left him staring at our dust. We weren't going to give much help to someone playing dead when, in reality, he was far from it. I kept my mouth shut, but I was chuckling to myself, thinking that fellow had just got a lesson on how the West was really won.

Every year around the last week of April we would trail a big herd of yearling heifers to Harbison, a forest allotment a few miles south of the Grand Canyon National Park. When I first went to work for Bill, the permit called for a few over 800 heifers, and then sometime in the '80s the Forest Service cut the permit to around 530 head. From Spider Web, the winter headquarters, to Harbison, was a three day drive. Two different places on the trail we would traverse a few miles of the Navajo Reservation and cross several different pastures within the CO Bar boundaries.

One year, sometime in the late '80s, I don't remember the year for sure, Bill hired a man the day before we were going to move camp to Lockwood. We would move on the second day of the trail drive and camp at Lockwood for several days, which would be the layover of the second day of the trail drive. We would gather bulls at Lockwood while we were there, as that was where the herd bulls ran during the winter. This fellow didn't help us the first day of the drive when we trailed the heifers from Spider Web to a place called Tommy Tank in the Mesa Butte pasture, about 15 miles to the west. If I remember correctly, the man stayed at Spider Web and shod three or four horses.

On the second day of the trail drive to Harbison, we were going to move camp, which included moving the remuda, which at that time of year was probably about 50 or 60 horses. The horses needed to be trailed up the exact same route we were taking with the heifers; although, the heifers had a 15-mile head start. One man would move the horses by himself, and the cook would move the chuck wagon; the rest of the crew, about eight men, would go to Tommy Tank and continue on with the heifers for the second leg of the journey.

We ate breakfast about 5:00 a.m., and everyone had their beds rolled up and were ready to go. About the time it was getting light, Bill, who had been particularly quiet that morning, got up and took his breakfast plate into the kitchen and put it in the roundup pan. He walked through the main room of the bunkhouse where everyone sat. He looked at the new fellow, who had been on the outfit a few hours, and said, "You're taking the horses." and he pointed out the window to the west. He went on, "Lockwood is that way." and with that and nothing more said, Bill stepped out the door and headed to the horse corral. That was a definite signal that the rest of us better follow suit, which we did. The new guy looked a little shell-shocked because he had not been given any further directions, advice, or description of the trail, the number of gates he would have to go through, or even the number of horses he would be trailing—nothing.

The wind was screaming bloody murder wiping out any tracks from the day before. We all saddled up, and waved goodbye to our new horse wrangler who was looking confused, and left him to fend for himself. Nobody gave him advice, but, actually, he didn't ask for any. Perhaps he was confident, but I never knew what went through his mind. I thought it was one of the craziest things I had ever seen, to tell a man who didn't know the country to do something that difficult, with no more than, "Lockwood is that way."

Lockwood is a pretty spot, the camp being situated on a hill in the fork of a nice canyon, with lots of limestone rock outcroppings and plenty of cedar and pinion trees scattered about. Up in the hills and canyons the wind wasn't nearly as bad as it was down at Spider Web and the wide open spaces. As the crow flies it's probably 18 miles from Spider Web to Lockwood, but by the trail we took with the livestock it's more like 24 or 25. We got there about noon with the cattle and watered them and turned them out in a holding pasture. The cook had coffee ready, and we were relaxing and wondering if we would ever see the horses again. About one o'clock a dust cloud could be seen coming up the canyon and, directly, here came the horses and our new man. Bill wasn't much on giving detailed directions but, evidently, he didn't need to be.

A lot of people talk about how cranky Bill was and how hard he was to work for. Bill could be cranky and difficult to be around, sure, but in a lot of ways he was very easy. He absolutely would not put up with nonsense. When he threw a roundup together, he wanted it held just right, not too tight and not too loose. He would put a man out away from a herd to hold a cut, and he wanted the fellow to position the cut in the exact spot where he had told him. He had a reason for everything he did, everything about cowboying and working cattle was a science to him, and he had given everything a great deal of thought, trying to figure out the best way to accomplish the task set before him. He was a perfectionist. When we branded he would look at his watch and time us, figuring out how long it took to brand calves. In his opinion a 10 man crew should brand a minimum of two calves a minute.

Bill was very good to kids if they wanted to be cowboys. No young boy who was a son of one of his employees went without a horse to ride if the kid acted interested. I know many good cowboys who worked for Bill when they were just young boys, and if they put out a little effort, he was very good to them all. He had no patience for a bragger or a phony, and if one showed up on the outfit they usually didn't last long.

One of my favorite memories was when my two boys were about eight and nine years old. Bill asked me to get them to help gather some cattle close to Spider Web. We gathered some cattle and held them up outside, and Bill was in the herd cutting cattle out. My boys, Everett and Clay, were on the backside of the herd and were both mounted on real good horses. Everett was on a horse called Beaver, and Clay, who was eight years old, was on a sorrel horse called Hotshot. A big fat dry cow broke out of the herd next to Clay and took off in a dead run. Clay pitched the slack to Hotshot who was running full bore right up in the cow's neck. You could tell things were fixing to get exciting, and I watched from the other side of the roundup hoping my youngest would survive what I knew was about to take place. Directly, Hotshot got an inch or two in front of the cow, and then she switched ends 180 degrees in a dead run. A cloud of dust covered everything for a second or two, and I figured my boy would be lying in a heap because he had failed to stay on when ole Hotshot switched directions. But when the dust settled, Clay and Hotshot were bringing the cow back to the roundup, perhaps a little too fast, but she hadn't got away. Clay was grinning from ear to ear, and the smile on his face was made possible because Bill Howell made sure my son had a good horse to ride.

Bill was the best cowman and manager I've ever known, but he only had a seventh-grade education. He had beautiful handwriting, but couldn't spell a four-letter word. Sometimes he would write the names of a mount of horses down on a piece of notebook paper and give it to a man so he could remember what his horses were. There was a big sorrel named Scar, and when he wrote the name down, along with four or five other names, and gave the list to a man he just hired, he almost ran the poor fellow off. Instead of writing Scar on the list, he misspelled the name and wrote Scare. The new man had heard of the outfit's reputation for having lots of buckers, and the

Bill Howell on Checkers, Spider Web, circa 1968

word Scare had an affect on him. He came to me quite agitated, asking if the horse named Scare lived up to his name.

One spring we gathered a big bunch of cows and were

trailing them into Spider Web from the east, starting in the Bardoni well area. Bill and Vic had an appointment to meet someone that afternoon in Flagstaff. He had also given the cook the word that we would be back at Spider Web at 12:00 noon to eat lunch. He and Vic left the crew with me in charge around 10:00 a.m., leaving me with orders to trail the herd of 300 cows into Spider Web and turn them loose on the west side of camp. He also reminded me that he had promised the cook we would be there at noon to eat. As he and Vic loped off, I thought to myself that there's no way we could make it into Spider Web with the herd of cattle before 1:00 p.m. at the earliest, but I said nothing.

About a mile and a half east of Spider Web we had to go through a fence, and when I loped up to the gate to open it, I noticed a small piece of paper folded up and stuck between the gate stick and wire bale that held the gate in place. It was a page ripped out of Bill's small tally book that he carried in his shirt pocket. He had realized that we wouldn't make it into camp by noon and had written me a note telling me to turn the cows loose and go to camp so we wouldn't make the cook mad by being late. The note read, "Trun the cows loose." He had more common sense, especially about economics, than most senators and congressman, but he couldn't spell a four-letter word.

The CO Bar Ranch bordered the Navajo Reservation for 50 miles. Twelve or fifteen miles of that boundary were on the Little Colorado River with no fence in between the ranch and the river. Indian livestock, encroaching and eating Babbitt grass, was a constant problem. Sometimes there were several hundred Indian horses running on the Babbitt side of the fence. Anytime you didn't have anything else to do you could always go chase some Indian horses or cattle back onto the reservation.

There were several Indians who stole from each other and had various tactics they used to accomplish this. The most common method was to ride around and castrate bull calves and earmark them, and then when a steer got big they branded him. Sometimes they just castrated them. There was a several year period when the shenanigans among the Indians hit epidemic proportions.

Corral full of wild Indian cattle roped on the Little Colorado River.

One day I was riding on the river and I counted 38 full grown steers, most of them unbranded. I also counted a number of maverick bulls and cows. The cattle stayed in the thick salt cedar thickets near the river in the day time and wandered out into the open and grazed at night. We had been catching a few of these cattle for years, in our spare time, and jerking them into a gooseneck, and hauling them to Spider Web. We would then contact the Indians and tell them to come and get them, and they would haul them to the auction. By doing this we kept the cattle thinned out and they were less of a problem eating Babbitt grass. When I reported to Bill that I had seen that many big steers in one day, he decided we should put out a little more effort gathering them and helping the Indians get rid of them.

There is a day in particular that stands out in my memory. About seven of us went to the river, arriving before sunup. It was about 20 degrees above zero when we got there. Besides Bill, Vic, and me, there were Jack Rodgers, Charles Kent, and Lane

Perry, and maybe another cowboy whom I can't remember. Bill and I went one direction, and Vic took everyone else in another, all of us being on the reservation side of the river. Bill and I rode out on a sandstone mesa, a mile or so from the river, and jumped a small two-year-old Hereford bull, roped him, and tied him down. He was unbranded and might have weighed 700 pounds.

We kept traveling farther away from the river, high-pointing and looking in every canyon and low place we could find, looking for more cattle. We were separated by several hundred yards when I rode up to the edge of the mesa we were on and looked down into the bottom of a big wide open draw and saw a dozen or so big cattle headed toward the river. They were trotting along at a good pace and had, no doubt, heard us from a mile or two away. I hollered at Bill, and gave him a wave, and then fell off the mesa in a dead run trying to reach the cattle before they got to the salt cedar thickets at the river's edge.

I was riding a five-year-old horse that I had broke several years earlier and named Jerky. As I got closer to the cattle, I could see there were at least six full grown steers among them. It was early spring, and the cattle were not as stout as they would have been in the late summer but were still in decent flesh. The last critter in the bunch was a big crossbred black steer that was as tall as my horse or possibly an inch or two taller. I ran up on him, and roped him around the neck, and pitched my slack over the right side of his hip, and drove Jerky on past him, and knocked him down. Jerky would work a rope plenty good, and I baled off and began tying his hind legs together. About the time I was getting my knot pulled tight, Bill ran past me and hollered a question; "Are you alright?" and I waved at him telling him to go on.

I got my rope off the steer and took off, hoping to catch another steer or two before they reached the river that was, at the most, a mile away. Bill was tying his pigging string around one's hind legs when I passed him, and I could tell he didn't need my help so I kept moving. We ended up catching and tying down three head apiece, all of them full grown and weighing at least a 1000 pounds, several of them weighing close to 1200. We never missed a loop and didn't require any help from the other man. When I roped the last steer, I caught him right on the edge of the river. The whole process didn't take more than three minutes. We had unsaddled our horses and were letting them blow when Vic and his crew rode up. We had seven critters tied down and they hadn't even seen a single cow. We were feeling pretty proud of ourselves and grinning from ear to ear.

Around 1990 a lot of changes were taking place among the stockholders of the Babbitt Ranches. John Babbitt and his generation were being replaced by younger members of the family, and; subsequently, a new direction and new ideas were inevitable. Bill was pointed to retirement, a process that took time, and wasn't without pain, at least on his part. He didn't go easily. Early in 1992, Bill and his wife Lynda, and their daughter Patricia, moved to Flagstaff.

Bill had been running some cows of his own on leased land for several years, and now that he was not on the Babbitt payroll he devoted all his time to taking care of his own cow herd. He had a ranch leased 40 miles east of Flagstaff and another 70 miles northwest of Flagstaff. One day his friend Doy Reidhead jokingly called his cattle operation Badly Scattered Cattle Company, and the name stuck, and from then on Bill referred to his personal business as "Badly Scattered." He was as successful at running his own affairs as he had been at running Babbitts' affairs, and he continued to prosper.

A year or so after retiring as Babbitts' ranch manager he had the second of two open heart surgeries. He didn't let the second slow him down anymore than the first and was soon back to working full time.

Around 2004 Bill started acting differently. One of the first strange things anyone noticed was when he showed up at Vic's house, threw his tally book down on the table and demanded some help figuring out "this mess." Bill Howell had never needed any help figuring out a tally book in his life. Within a few months he was diagnosed with Alzheimer's disease.

In the spring of 2007, the Arizona Cowpuncher's Reunion Association had a roping in the indoor arena at the Apache Gold

Casino in Globe, Arizona. One of the events was a century roping, and Bill had entered with Tom Bill Johnson, who is a professional level roper. When the announcer called their names, telling them to ride into the box, Bill rode into the header's box; although, he and Tom Bill had agreed beforehand that Bill would heel. Tom Bill very gracefully told Bill that he needed to get on the other side of the chute in the heeler's box. Though Bill acted confused, he said okay and did what Tom Bill told him to do. Tom Bill called for the steer and roped him by the head, and when he turned him Bill roped two feet. Forty-five minutes later, when it was time to rope their second steer, Bill rode in the header's box again, and Tom Bill politely led Bill over to the heeler's box and did so without embarrassing him.

Four months later the big Cowpuncher's Reunion Rodeo was held at Williams, Arizona. One evening Bill's youngest son, Tom, had a barbeque at his camp near the rodeo grounds. It was a big get-together, and by chance I got paired up with Bill. We let down the tailgate of my pickup and used it for a table, laying our plates full of good barbeque on it, and stood there together eating. I wasn't sure if he knew who I was, but he was comfortable being with me and we visited. He couldn't keep the same train of thought going for a long time but would talk one short sentence at a time. He told fleeting stories from 50 years earlier but seemed to remember nothing recent. He mentioned what a mean son of a gun his father had been, and at one point I thought he might cry. In respect I let him talk about whatever he wanted to talk about. It didn't matter to me if he had Alzheimer's. I wasn't going to tell him what to do.

At that time I owned a small horse we all called Squish. I had bought the horse, which came off the Navajo Reservation, from one of Everett's bronc riding friends named Brett Crowser. Squish stood an inch under 14 hands and weighed about 950 pounds. I had bought the horse for my grandkids and had hauled him to the reunion so they could use him in the kid's gymkhana the reunion has every year. It was the morning after Tom's barbeque, and when the gymkhana ended it became my job to take Squish back to our camp, and unsaddle him, and put him

Bill Howell and Everett Ashurst visiting at the CO Bar Ranch.

back in our portable horse corral.

About the time I got the saddle off of Squish's back, I looked up and saw Bill riding toward me. He was wandering aimlessly around the rodeo grounds on Chip, the last good rope horse he had trained. When he got 15 feet away from where Squish and I stood, he looked at the very short horse and then at me. In a flash of lucidity that is common among people afflicted with Alzheimer's, he grinned and said very plainly, "You having a hard time getting on these days, Ed?"

Startled at his wit I answered him and said, "Yeah, I guess so, Bill."

He grinned from ear to ear for several seconds, and then in an instant his face turned blank, and he turned the bay horse and pointed him down the road. I watched him ride off. The man had influenced me more than any other since my seventeenth birthday. His chest was slightly forward and his shoulders square, and I wondered if he was looking for another cow to cut, or a steer to rope, or maybe a new gate to ride through. He rode toward the back of the rodeo arena, and for a moment time seemed to stand still while he disappeared among the diesel pickups and aluminum horse trailers, and became nothing more than a memory… a good one.

ᔥᔥ

About the Artist

ᔥᔥ

I have always been fascinated by these three things: ridin', ropin', and paintin'. I find many things similar in these three art forms. The challenges are always present in all three. Nobody rides every horse, nobody catches every cow, and nobody makes a masterpiece every time. I am satisfied to concentrate on the art form of painting, drawing and sculpture at the present. Sharpening the fundamentals will keep me busy through this lifetime. I love the problems of creating a picture. This is a means of communications that has been around since the first cave wall artist. Expressing oneself is always a challenge, but it can be hopeless if you don't have anything to say. My life has been a combination of the people I have worked with and their connection to God's Country. Not to mention his animals. The stories are endless and all are worthy of consideration for a painting or drawing. I would like for all of my work to be believable by the viewer, and enjoyed free of charge. *Mike Capron*

ಬಿಲಿ
About the Author
ಬಿಲಿ

Author, Ed Ashurst. Photo by Kathy McCraine.

Ed Ashurst was born in Arizona and has ridden on at least seven thousand square mile of range land in four different states gathering cattle and horses.

Made in United States
Troutdale, OR
11/23/2024

25163885R00136